# Inequality and the Future of Canadian Society

## S.D. Clark

The University of Toronto's Department of Sociology was established in 1963. Samuel Delbert (S.D.) Clark (1910–2003) was its founding chair.

Clark was born in Lloydmister, Alberta, and attended the University of Saskatchewan, the London School of Economics, McGill University and the University of Toronto. He analyzed the transformation of successive Canadian frontiers from socially disorganized settlements into organized societies. He then conducted research on how economic change in Canada resulted in inequality as reflected in patterns of residential segregation. His books include *The Canadian Manufacturers Association* (1939), *The Social Development of Canada* (1942), *Church and Sect in Canada* (1948), *Movements of Political Protest in Canada* (1959), *The Developing Canadian Community* (1962), *The Suburban Society* (1966), *Canadian Society in Historical Perspective* (1976) and *The New Urban Poor* (1978).

Clark served as president of the Canadian Political Science Association, honorary president of the Canadian Sociology and Anthropology Association and president of the Royal Society of Canada. He was awarded the J.B. Tyrell Historical Medal, became a foreign honorary member of the American Academy of Arts and Sciences and an Officer of the Order of Canada, and received honorary degrees from half a dozen Canadian universities.

In 1999, Clark's son, William Edmund (Ed) Clark, endowed the S.D. Clark Chair in Sociology at the University of Toronto in honour of his father.

# Inequality and the Future of Canadian Society

## PROCEEDINGS OF THE FIRST
## S.D. CLARK SYMPOSIUM
## ON THE FUTURE OF CANADIAN SOCIETY

EDITED BY
## Robert Brym

Rock's Mills Press
Oakville, Ontario

PUBLISHED BY

**ROCK'S MILLS PRESS**
www.rocksmillspress.com

CREDITS FOR ILLUSTRATIONS AND FIGURES: The cover image is of a Banksy mural mounted in December 2011; Simon Balson/Alamy. Figure 1.2 is based on Guppy and Luongo (2015). Figure 2.1 is based on data from Statistics Canada (2016). Figure 2.2 is based on data from OECD (2016a, 2016b). Figure 3.1 is based on International Monetary Fund (2013: 37). Figure 3.2 is based on Saez and Veall (2003:90). Figure 4.1 is based on Alexander Hertel-Fernandez and Cathie Jo Martin, "How employers and conservatives shaped the modern tax state," unpublished paper, Boston University, 2015. Figures 5.1 and 5.2 are based on OECD, 2016a. Figures 6.1 and 6.2 are based on Survey of Young Canadians, 2010–2011.

For information, contact customer.service@rocksmillspress.com.
Library and Archives Canada Cataloguing in Publication data is available from the publisher.

# Contents

# List of Tables

# List of Figures

Inequality and the Future
of Canadian Society

CHAPTER ONE

# Inequality and the Future of Canadian Society

## Robert Brym

S.D. Clark (1910–2003) was the first chair of the Department of Sociology at the University of Toronto. During the first three decades of his career he analyzed the transformation of successive Canadian frontiers from socially disorganized settlements into organized societies. He then conducted research on how economic change in Canada resulted in inequality as reflected in patterns of residential segregation. *The New Urban Poor* was the title of Clark's last book, published nearly 40 years ago (Clark, 1978). The first S.D. Clark Symposium on the Future of Canadian Society, held at the University of Toronto in October 2015, picked up where Clark left off by focusing on income inequality—and its implications for tax and gender policy. This volume contains the revised proceedings of the symposium.

Before introducing the symposium's themes and dramatis personae, two observations about the state of income inequality studies today are in order (Banting and Myles, 2015: 511–15):

1. In Canada, inequality in *market* income (from earnings and investments) started rising in the early 1980s, increased rapidly in the 1990s and levelled off in the 2000s. Taxes and transfer payments held the rise in check until the mid-1990s, at which time cuts to employment insurance benefits and social assistance payments caused income inequality *after taxes and transfer payments* to start rising. Since about 2000, inequality in income after taxes and transfer payments has remained approximately stable.

2. Between 1982 and 2010, the top 10 percent of tax filers received nearly all income gains in the country. The percentage of the population earning less than half the median income (the

proportion of Canadians classified as low-income earners) has remained steady at about 13 percent since the mid-'90s. However, the mean income of the lower middle class has been hit hard due mainly to deindustrialization and technological change.

If researchers can agree on this much, they are at loggerheads when it comes to discussing policy issues regarding the income distribution. To illustrate the problem, allow me to refer first to the famous fifteenth-century Borgia World Map, presently housed in the Vatican library (The Borgia World Map, n.d.). To modern eyes, the map portrays an unrecognizable world. The south is at the top. Parts of continents are missing. In places, mountains symbolize coastlines. And in the upper left quadrant we see the figures of three enormous men, a serpent, and an inscription in Latin that reads as follows: "Here also are huge men having horns four feet long, and there are serpents also of such magnitude that they can eat an ox whole."

I do not think I will exaggerate greatly by claiming that policy discussion concerning income inequality resembles a sort of updated Borgia map (Figure 1.1). Consider first the two X's on the map. They represent what students of income inequality know with certainty. If income inequality is too low or too high, we are likely to observe outcomes that most people consider undesirable. If income inequality is too low, we have a Soviet-type society in which people lack the motivation to work hard, as a result of which the standard of living languishes. As a Russian quip from the 1970s put it, "You pretend to pay us and we pretend to work." If income inequality is too high, we have England in the early years of the Industrial Revolution, which witnessed poverty so debilitating magistrates in rural Berkshire demanded that the state intervene. They felt compelled to devise a means-tested sliding scale of wage supplements funded by landowners (Polanyi, 1944).

What students of income inequality debate is the shape of the curve connecting the two X's. Some analysts hold that the curve is negatively skewed. From their point of view, a high level of income inequality is desirable because it motivates people to work hard, creating jobs, resulting in a higher standard of living for all and, eventually, sharply reducing absolute poverty.

Other analysts hold that the curve is positively skewed. From their point of view, when income inequality rises beyond a certain low level, bad things start happening—in particular, we may witness less upward mobility and political stability, more crime, slower economic growth, declining levels of health, trust, and happiness, and a trend toward plutocracy (Kenworthy, 2015).

The ranks of those who endorse the positively skewed curve have swollen in recent years. They include the authors of all of

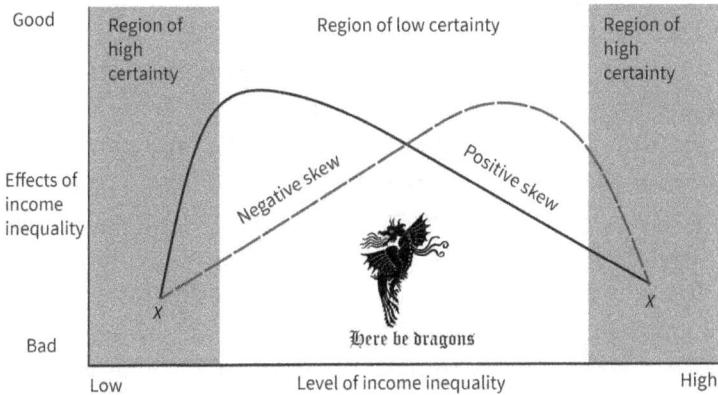

Figure 1.1.  A New "Borgia Map" of the Effects of Income Inequality

the papers in this volume. Even economists who work for the World Bank and, perhaps less surprisingly, TD Canada Trust, have recently issued reports decrying some of the effects of increasing income inequality (Craig & Fong, 2014; Dabla-Norris et al., 2015). Nonetheless, debate over the shape of the curve remains so heated that I feel obliged to attach an appropriate warning at the bottom of my updated Borgia map.

In this volume's first paper, Robert Andersen, dean of Social Science at Western University, takes issue with an important implication of the negatively skewed curve. He first demonstrates that, among the 34 democratic market economies comprising the Organization of Economic Cooperation and Development (OECD), prosperity and inequality are inversely proportional; the richest countries are the most equal. This finding leads Andersen to inquire into the kinds of tax, education and labour policies that allow prosperity and egalitarianism to coexist. Instructively, he discovers that countries like Denmark combine low corporate tax rates with high personal and consumption taxes. Low corporate tax rates incentivize businesses not to migrate to low-wage countries. High personal and consumption taxes allow the government to offer unemployed workers a high level of economic security and relevant job retraining. Government, business and labour routinely plan the education and training of workers to ensure that the labour needs of the economy are met. Andersen recognizes that Canada's political makeup presents obstacles to the development of such policies. However, he also convincingly establishes the existence of opportunities to learn from countries like Denmark.

Lars Osberg, McCulloch Professor of Economics at Dalhousie University, forcefully tugs at another aspect of the negatively skewed curve that supposedly characterizes the relationship between inequality and desirable outcomes. Many reporters and academics, and, it seems, pretty well all businesspeople, assume that if the top marginal income tax rate edges above 50 percent, top earners will begin questioning whether it makes sense to work hard and risk investing. Raise the top marginal income tax rate much higher, and businesspeople will purportedly consider leaving the country altogether for more hospitable tax environments. Osberg employs hard logic and evidence to undermine this argument. He first shows that Canada's top marginal income tax rate is relatively low compared to the past and to other jurisdictions. He then demonstrates how a variety of regulations and weak enforcement allow wealthy individuals to minimize their taxes. Next he asks whether high income earners would really work less hard if the top tax rate were raised. He shows that the number of hours worked actually accounts for only a tiny fraction of the variation in income among Canada's top 1 percent of earners. The top 0.01 percent of income earners do not work much harder than those who barely make it into the top 1 percent. It follows that lowering earnings by raising the top tax rate would not have as much of an effect on hours worked as is often imagined. Nor is it likely that raising the top marginal tax rate to, say, 65 percent would cause a mass out-migration of wealthy Canadians. American and Swiss research on neighbouring jurisdictions shows practically no migration when one jurisdiction raises the top marginal income tax rate, even when the jurisdictions in question are in the same metropolitan area. Osberg calculates that raising Canada's top marginal income tax rate to 65 percent would increase annual tax revenue from all sources by all levels of government between 8.9 percent and 14.8 percent. He makes a strong case for the rationality of such a move.

In a brief reflection on the papers by Andersen and Osberg, John Myles, emeritus professor of sociology at the University of Toronto, presents a disturbing paradox: "Countries with high levels of taxation and social spending rely mainly on regressive payroll and consumption taxes on labour while taxes on capital are modest. The low-spending US wins the beauty contest for the most progressive tax system." Myles does not dispute Osberg's point that there is plenty of room for increasing the taxation of wealthy Canadians. Nor does he take issue with Andersen's claim that Danish egalitarianism benefits the entire society. However, Myles does make the persuasive argument that, to get to Denmark, the Canadian middle class must pay much higher taxes and be convinced that the public benefits of increased taxation are worth the decline in private consumption. How this can be achieved politically is an open and troubling question.

The second part of this volume shifts focus from tax policy to gender policy. On this front we have witnessed a revolution over the past century (Figure 1.2). Between 1921 and 2013, women's participation in the paid labour force rose from a fifth to three-fifths of the female population over the age of 14. For people working full-year, full-time in the paid labour force, the ratio of women's to men's earnings increased from 58 percent to 76 percent between 1967 and 2011. From 1920 to 2011, the ratio of women to men receiving undergraduate and first professional degrees jumped from 20 percent to 160 percent. Between 1920 and 2015, the ratio of women to men serving as Members of Parliament rose from 0 percent to 26 percent. And from 1970 to 1999, the gender gap in child care and housework for 20- to 59-year olds fell from 3.3 hours to 2.0 hours per day.

Equally telling is the degree to which progress in women's economic opportunity, educational attainment, political power, and the division of domestic labour has stalled in the last few years. Women's participation in the paid labour force has barely budged for a quarter of a century and has declined recently. Improvements in pay equity and representation in Parliament, and gender convergence in the domestic division of labour, have slowed or reversed over the past five to ten years (Guppy & Luongo, 2015).

The adoption of neoliberal policies seems to be largely responsible for the slowdown. The ruling Conservative party favoured the entrenchment of the traditional nuclear family, so while it was in power from 2006 to 2015 it introduced a child tax benefit, income

Figure 1.2  Change in Measures of Gender Inequality, Canada

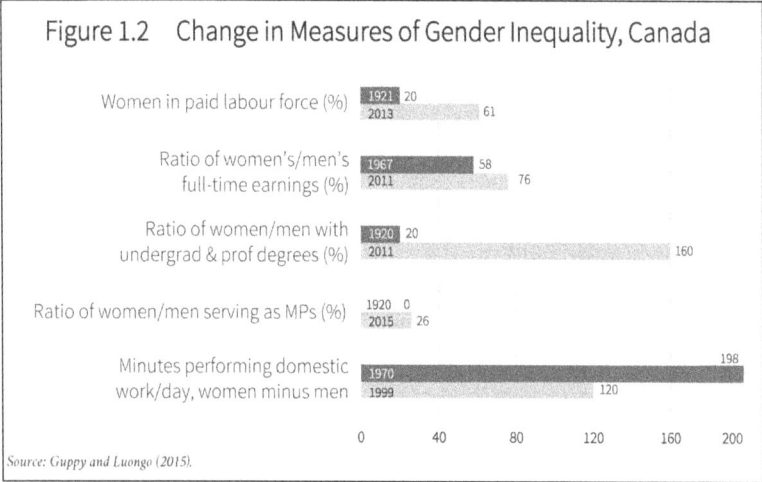

| | | |
|---|---|---|
| Women in paid labour force (%) | 1921 | 20 |
| | 2013 | 61 |
| Ratio of women's/men's full-time earnings (%) | 1967 | 58 |
| | 2011 | 76 |
| Ratio of women/men with undergrad & prof degrees (%) | 1920 | 20 |
| | 2011 | 160 |
| Ratio of women/men serving as MPs (%) | 1920 | 0 |
| | 2015 | 26 |
| Minutes performing domestic work/day, women minus men | 1970 | 198 |
| | 1999 | 120 |

0    40    80    120    160    200

Source: Guppy and Luongo (2015).

splitting between spouses with children under the age of eighteen and other policy mechanisms that disproportionately benefited high income earners and incentivized women to stay out of the paid labour force. These are precisely the opposite of the kinds of policies that would promote a higher level of gender and income equality—chief among them, high-quality, universally accessible child care (Esping-Andersen, 2009).

Ito Peng, professor of sociology and director of the Centre for Global Social Policy at the University of Toronto, provides a useful comparative overview of factors responsible for the development of welfare state policies that affect gender inequality. The overall level of state spending is strongly associated with relatively low gender inequality—but only if one compares rich and poor countries. As Peng shows, among rich countries, the correlation between state spending and gender equality is weak. What matters more is the way policy makers conceptualize the roles that women play in society. Moving toward gender equality requires the implementation of policies that identify women not as mothers, not even as workers, but as workers with disproportionate and particular household responsibilities, especially those involving child care. Only if women are identified in this way can policy makers design state programs that enable women to approach equality with men in economic and political life. Even countries that are not rich can make substantial progress toward gender equality by implementing programs that adopt such a model. But countries that are rich, like Canada, can find progress toward gender equality stymied by failure to adopt an "adult worker household" model, which assumes that the great majority of women and men will work most of their adult lives and contribute equally to domestic labour.

One important program based on this model is universally accessible, strongly state-subsidized, state-regulated, high-quality child care. Disadvantaged women in particular tend to benefit strongly from child-care systems of this type in terms of their ability to receive a higher education and work for pay. Children, particularly those from disadvantaged families, also tend to benefit strongly in terms of positive cognitive and behavioural outcomes.

Gordon Cleveland of the Department of Management at the University of Toronto Scarborough comprehensively and critically reviews a large research literature on this subject. While he arrives at the conclusions I have just summarized, he finds it necessary to qualify them in important ways. Child-care systems that are not designed to be especially accessible to low-income parents and their children often do not have the expected effects on gender inequality or child outcomes. In fact, the introduction of a state-subsidized child care system in which there is an insufficient number of highly trained child-care workers (as in Quebec) can have negative consequences for some children, particularly boys from disadvantaged families. The benefits of child care for children are most evident if they do not begin such programs before the age of two. These and other findings lead Cleveland to make pointed policy recommendations as Canadians contemplate the improvement of child-care services in Quebec and the expansion of child-care services in the rest of the country.

Emily Laxer, a postdoctoral student at the University of Michigan, concludes the discussion of gender policy and gender inequality by reminding us that the formulation and effective implementation of gender equalization policies depend heavily on the parliamentary representation of women who are strongly inclined to promote gender equality—including women who are members of disadvantaged racial minority groups. Without more such representation, welfare state policies are unlikely to increase benefits for racialized women who are overrepresented in the most precarious, low-income positions in the Canadian labour market.

· · · · ·

On 27 August 2015, in the midst of the Canadian federal election campaign, Justin Trudeau announced that the Liberals intended to run budget deficits, doubling infrastructure spending to create jobs and stimulate growth. Just ten days earlier he had promised a tax bracket with a higher marginal rate for Canadians earning more than $200,000 a year and a reduced-rate bracket for those earning between $44,700 and $89,401 a year. These were audacious pledges. They placed the Liberals to the left of the New Democratic Party in the minds of many Canadian voters. By most accounts, they were the policy promises that won the Liberals the election.

However, the evidence-based papers in this volume provocatively suggest that Liberal policies, although welcome, will do little to ameliorate growing inequality in Canadian society. The contributors argue that more fundamental policy changes are needed. These reforms relate to taxation, child care, postsecondary education, worker training and political representation. Moreover—and conventional wisdom notwithstanding—the evidence assembled and the analyses undertaken in this volume suggest that such reforms promise to increase prosperity. The contributors are well aware of the political challenges that make such reforms difficult to achieve. Their clear-minded analyses nonetheless elevate the discussion to a more realistic plane for Canadians who support an equality agenda.

# References

Alexander, Craig & Francis Fong. 2014. "The case for leaning against income inequality in Canada." Special Report, TD Economics. http://www.td.com/document/PDF/economics/special/income_inequality.pdf.

Banting, Keith and John Myles. 2015. "Framing the New Inequality: The Politics of Income Distribution in Canada." In David A. Green, W. Craig Riddell and France St-Hilaire, eds. *Income Inequality: The Canadian Story.* http://irpp.org/wp-content/uploads/2016/01/aots5-banting-myles.pdf.

The Borgia World Map. n.d. http://cartographic-images.net/Cartographic_Images/237_The_Borgia_World_Map.html.

CBC. 2015. "Justin Trudeau's Liberals to form majority government." http://www.cbc.ca/news2/interactives/results-2015/.

Clark, S. D. 1978. *The New Urban Poor.* Toronto: McGraw-Hill Ryerson.

Dabla-Norris, Era, Kalpana Kochhar, Frantisek Ricka, Nujin Suphaphiphat & Evridiki Tsounta (with contributions from Preya Sharma & Veronique Salins). 2015. "Causes and consequences of income inequality: a global perspective." Strategy, Policy, and Review Department, International Monetary Fund. https://www.imf.org/external/pubs/ft/sdn/2015/sdn1513.pdf

Esping-Andersen, Gøsta. 2009. *The Incomplete Revolution: Adapting to Women's New Roles.* Cambridge, UK: Polity.

Guppy, Neil & Nicole Luongo. 2015. "The rise and stall of Canada's gender-equity revolution." *Canadian Review of Sociology* 52, 3: 241–65.

Kenworthy, Lane. 2015. "Is income inequality harmful?" http://lanekenworthy.net/is-income-inequality-harmful/.

Polanyi, Karl. 1944. *The Great Transformation: The Political and Economic Origins of Our Time.* New York: Farrar & Rinehart.

# CHAPTER TWO

# What Can Canada Learn from Europe? Policies to Promote Low Income Inequality and High Prosperity

## Robert Andersen

High income inequality negatively influences business, government and civil society. For example, countries with high inequality tend to exhibit low levels of general social trust (Uslaner, 2002; Uslaner & Brown, 2005), trust in political institutions (Grabb, Andersen, Hwang &Milligan, 2009), trust in business (Stiglitz, 2012; 2015), tolerance of out-groups (Andersen & Fetner, 2008; Milligan, Andersen & Brym, 2014) and support for democracy (Andersen, 2012). Moreover, countries with high inequality tend to be characterized by a poor match between educational qualifications and labour market outcomes (Andersen & Van de Werfhorst 2010) and low social mobility (Mitnik, Cumberworth & Grusky, 2013), both of which act as barriers against firms hiring the most qualified and talented people. Within firms, high inequality, as measured by the ratio of CEO-to-average-employee compensation, negatively influences firm profitability and value (Bebchuck, Cremers & Peyer, 2011).

With one eye on Europe, this chapter considers how Canadian policy makers might consider tackling economic inequality in ways that produce favourable outcomes for both individuals and businesses. I start by summarizing the pattern of income inequality in Canada and common interpretations for its rise over the past several decades. I then compare Canada to other rich countries to identify social and economic policies that might reduce inequality and increase productivity. I argue that the key to decreasing inequality in Canada lies with ensuring that conditions are good for business, not just for individuals. Utilizing data from the OECD and the World Bank, and contrary to much conventional wisdom, I provide evidence that low inequality and economic prosperity are not incompatible. In fact, the most equal countries in the world are among the most productive. Concomitantly, these countries have policies that tend to be highly favourable for business. I conclude that Canada would be well served by instituting policies that facilitate profitability and decrease differences in incomes.

## Income Inequality in Canada: How Does It Compare to Other Countries?

Three noteworthy observations can be made about the trend in income inequality in Canada since the late 1970s: (1) market-generated inequality has risen drastically (Franette & Milligan, 2009; Heisz, 2007); (2) much of the rise is due to substantial gains among the top income earners (Saez & Veal 2003; 2005; Fortin, et al., 2012); and (3) inequality has risen, albeit less dramatically, even after taking taxes and government transfers into account (Andersen & McIvor, 2014). Figure 2.1 uses Statistics Canada (2016) data to illustrate trends in the Gini coefficient for household incomes in Canada from 1976 to 2013. (The Gini coefficient has a theoretical range of 0 if every household in a country earns the same income and 1 if one household earns all of the income). We see a striking increase in market-generated income inequality, with the Gini coefficient rising from 0.38 in 1976 to 0.44 in 2013. A similar trend of lesser magnitude exists after taxes and transfers are considered; the Gini coefficient was as low at 0.29 in the late 1970s and rose to 0.32 by 2013. The failure of social policy to keep pace with changes in the market is most noticeable in the 1990s, a period marked by government cutbacks in an attempt to tackle the public debt (Ferris & Winer, 2007; Tupper, 1993).

Much of the rise in inequality in Canada reflects the globalization of economic markets. The liberalization of trade that has been facilitated by the North American Free Trade Agreement (NAFTA) has allowed firms to easily move production to countries with lower wages. This trend has resulted in the replacement of many high-paying manufacturing jobs by low-paying service jobs, most of which are not unionized (Cranford et al., 2003; Golden &

Wallerstein, 2006; Vosko, 2006). So-called skills-based technological change has also been said to contribute to growing inequality (Johnson 1997, Jorgenson 2001, Katz 1999). Supposedly, technological innovation, especially developments in computing, has led to a high-wage premium for people with skills that the global economy requires. Those who lack the training required to compete in this new market have purportedly been left behind. Proponents of this view argue that educational qualifications will eventually catch up and a new equilibrium will be reached, resulting in declining inequality. While skills-based technological change may explain some of the growth in inequality, evidence suggests that it is not as important as originally thought (Card & Dinardo, 2002).

Global competition also led to significant increases in income at the top of the income distribution (Saez & Veal, 2003; 2005). As corporations increasingly compete globally for CEOs and other talented people, salaries rise. The top one percent of earners received less than eight percent of all income in Canada just after World War II but their share of income rose to well over 12 percent by 2012 (Fortin, et al., 2012). The top one percent now receives nearly as large a share of the income distribution as it did during the Great Depression. A large part of these gains result from a tremendous increase in CEO compensation. Adjusted for inflation, average compensation for Canada's top CEOs increased by an astonishing ten times between 1980 and 2010, when it reached $3 million (Gelinas & Baillargeon, 2013).

Demographic change has also played a role in the rise of market income inequality. Particularly important is the increase in single-parent and dual-income families (Heisz, 2007; Picot & Myles, 1995). In contrast to a few decades ago, when a traditional family was characterized by two parents and a single income earner, most Canadian families today have two income earners. On the other hand, family dissolution is now much more common. A new gap in household incomes has thus been created between those with two incomes and those with one. The gap has been accentuated by a growth in marital homogamy (i.e., like marrying like) in Canada since 1980, especially among the highly educated who tend to be well-off economically (Hou & Myles, 2008).

Apart from increased market-generated income inequality,

Canada has also witnessed significant growth in income inequality after taxes and transfers. Governments were slow—perhaps unwilling—to respond to the rise in market inequality in the early 1990s (Finnie & Irvine, 2011; Heisz, 2007; Frenette et al., 2009). Instead, concern focused largely on spending cuts with the goal of decreasing Canada's public debt and decreasing taxes (Green-

Figure 2.1. Gini Coefficients for Household Income,
before and after taxes and transfers, Canada, 1976 to 2013

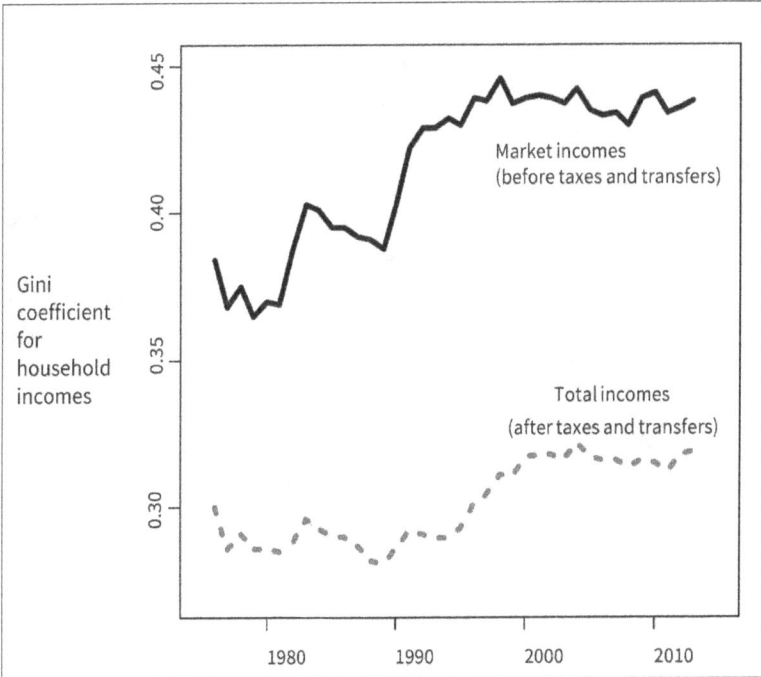

Source: Statistics Canada, 2016.

spon & Wilson-Smith, 1996; Osberg and Fortin, 1998; Minister of Finance 2006). As a result, the 1990s were marked by a rapid and continual decline in spending on social assistance and unemployment insurance (Andersen & McIvor, 2014; Battle et al., 2005; Banting, 2006). Simply put, social spending failed to counter the large growth in income inequality generated by the market.

How does inequality in Canada compare to inequality in other rich countries? Specifically, how is inequality across rich countries associated with prosperity, and where does Canada fit in the picture? To begin answering these questions, we turn to Table 2.1 (p.

16), which displays data on the level of household income inequality measured by the Gini coefficient (OECD, 2016a), GDP per capita (OECD, 2016b) and measures of various policies for the 34 OECD countries. These policy measures, which will be used later to predict income inequality and GDP per capita, are as follows:

1. **Social spending.** Measures total public social spending related to all financial flows from public bodies for social purposes. Measured as a percentage of GDP. Data were derived from the OECD's (2016c) Social Expenditure Database.

2. **Free tertiary education.** Coded 1 if the country has no tuition for public tertiary educational institutions, 0 if there are tuition fees. Information on tuition was obtained from the OECD (2015a).

3. **Active labour market policies.** Total public spending on labour market programs related to employment services, job training, hiring subsidies, direct job creation in the public sector and unemployment benefits. Data were derived from the OECD's (2016d) public spending database.

4. **Ease of doing business ranking.** This measure was taken from the World Bank Group's (2016) database on business regulations. Countries are ranked from lowest to highest, with low ranks representing extreme ease of doing business due to a regulatory environment that is conducive to the start-up and operation of a firm. Ranks were determined by aggregating 10 indicators related to ease of obtaining permits, costs of utilities and ease of obtaining credit, taxes, trade and contracts.

5. **Corporate taxes.** Measured as a percentage of profits. Corporate tax rates often differ within countries according to jurisdiction. In such cases, the highest rate is used. Data were taken from the OECD's (2016e) database on Tax Statistics.

6. **Sales or consumption taxes.** Measured as a percentage of the cost of the product or service. Consumption tax rates sometimes differ within countries according to jurisdiction. The highest rate is used. Data for this measure were taken from the OECD's (2016e) database on Tax Statistics.

Table 2.1 ranks countries in ascending order according to level of income inequality. The row containing data for Canada is shaded to permit easy identification. We start by focusing on the first two columns, which display the Gini coefficient and GDP per capita for the 34 OECD countries. Note first that European countries, especially countries in Northern Europe, tend to have the lowest level of income inequality, with Denmark leading the way. Second, Canada falls near the middle of the 34 countries in terms of income inequality, though it is closer to the USA and the UK than it is to Denmark. This fact is not surprising given that Canada is a liberal welfare state characterized by a fairly open market economy and, at best, moderate redistribution policies (Banting, 2005; Esping-Andersen, 1993; Myles, 1998). Third, there appears to be little relationship between a country's Gini coefficient and GDP per capita. Thus, Denmark has a GDP per capita similar to that of Canada but a much lower level of income inequality. There are also several countries with high income inequality and low GDP per capita.

Figure 2.2 more clearly demonstrates the relationship between the Gini coefficient and GDP per capita. It dispels the myth that reducing inequality would lower prosperity. If anything, there is a negative relationship between inequality and prosperity; as inequality rises, countries tend to be less prosperous. Both the correlation between the two variables ($r=-0.379$) and the lowess smooth (locally weighted regression curve) support this observation. Consistent with this relationship, Denmark enjoys not only the lowest income inequality in the world but also the highest rank in the 2016 Forbes Ranking of Best Countries for Business. Low-inequality Norway, Sweden and Finland are not far behind Denmark in their friendliness toward business (Forbes, 2016). Canada ranks relatively high as the world's seventh-best country for business. Despite its reputation for capitalism and big business, the USA, with the highest level of inequality among the world's rich countries, ranks much lower as the twenty-second-best country for business. In short, low inequality and economic prosperity are not incompatible. I will later provide evidence that inequality can be reduced while increasing prosperity. In other words, it is possible to implement policies that simultaneously benefit businesses and labour.

## Table 2.1
### Economic prosperity (GDP per capita), income inequality (Gini coefficient for household incomes) and various policy initiatives, OECD countries.
### Countries listed in ascending order by level of income inequality.

| Country | Gini co-efficient (house-hold in-comes) | GDP per capita (US dollars) | Social spend-ing (% of GDP) | Free ter-tiary tuition | Active labour poli-cies (per-cent of GDP) | Ease of doing business ranking (1= easiest) | Cor-porate tax rate (top) | Sales taxes (top) |
|---|---|---|---|---|---|---|---|---|
| Denmark | 0.25 | 46 000 | 30.1 | Yes | 3.49 | 3 | 22.0 | 25.0 |
| Norway | 0.25 | 65 705 | 22.0 | Yes | 0.83 | 9 | 25.0 | 25.0 |
| Slovakia | 0.25 | 28 327 | 18.4 | No | 0.63 | 25 | 22.0 | 20.0 |
| Slovenia | 0.25 | 30 405 | 23.7 | Yes | 1.17 | 29 | 17.0 | 22.0 |
| Czech Republic | 0.26 | 31 188 | 20.6 | Yes | 0.55 | 36 | 19.0 | 21.0 |
| Finland | 0.26 | 40 684 | 31.0 | Yes | 2.63 | 10 | 20.0 | 24.0 |
| Iceland | 0.26 | 43 993 | 16.5 | Yes | -- | 19 | 20.0 | 24.0 |
| Belgium | 0.27 | 43 724 | 30.7 | No | 2.76 | 43 | 33.0 | 21.0 |
| Sweden | 0.27 | 45 298 | 28.1 | Yes | 2.03 | 8 | 22.0 | 25.0 |
| Austria | 0.28 | 47 693 | 28.4 | No | 2.16 | 21 | 25.0 | 20.0 |
| Netherlands | 0.28 | 48 256 | 24.7 | No | 2.82 | 28 | 25.0 | 21.0 |
| Germany | 0.29 | 46 394 | 25.8 | Yes | 1.67 | 15 | 29.7 | 19.0 |
| Hungary | 0.29 | 25 061 | 22.1 | -- | 1.12 | 42 | 19.0 | 27.0 |
| Switzerland | 0.29 | 59 536 | 19.4 | No | 1.19 | 26 | 17.9 | 8.0 |
| Ireland | 0.30 | 49 402 | 21.0 | No | 3.09 | 17 | 12.5 | 23.0 |
| Korea | 0.30 | 33 395 | 10.4 | No | 0.57 | 4 | 24.2 | 10.0 |
| Luxembourg | 0.30 | 98 110 | 23.5 | -- | 1.51 | 61 | 28.0 | 17.0 |
| Poland | 0.30 | 24 952 | 20.6 | -- | 0.76 | 25 | 19.0 | 23.0 |
| France | 0.31 | 39 357 | 31.9 | No | -- | 27 | 55.0 | 20.0 |
| Canada | 0.32 | 45 025 | 21.6 | No | 0.80 | 14 | 31.0 | 15.0 |
| Australia | 0.33 | 46 281 | 19.0 | No | 0.87 | 13 | 30.0 | 10.0 |
| Italy | 0.33 | 35 419 | 28.6 | No | 1.99 | 45 | 27.5 | 22.0 |
| New Zealand | 0.33 | 38 113 | 20.8 | No | 0.64 | 2 | 28.0 | 15.0 |
| Estonia | 0.34 | 28 111 | 16.3 | -- | 0.68 | 16 | 0.0 | 20.0 |
| Greece | 0.34 | 26 795 | 24.0 | -- | -- | 60 | 58.0 | 23.0 |
| Japan | 0.34 | 36 581 | 23.1 | No | 0.47 | 34 | 38.0 | 8.0 |
| Portugal | 0.34 | 28 760 | 25.2 | No | 2.16 | 23 | 25.0 | 23.0 |
| Spain | 0.34 | 33 638 | 26.8 | No | -- | 33 | 25.0 | 21.0 |
| UK | 0.35 | 40 227 | 21.7 | No | 0.54 | 6 | 20.0 | 20.0 |
| Israel | 0.38 | 33 718 | 15.5 | -- | -- | 53 | 25.0 | 17.0 |
| USA | 0.40 | 54 353 | 19.2 | No | 0.35 | 7 | 47.0 | 11.7 |
| Turkey | 0.41 | 19 610 | 12.5 | -- | -- | 55 | 20.0 | 18.0 |
| Mexico | 0.48 | 18 046 | 7.9 | Yes | 0.01 | 38 | 30.0 | 16.0 |
| Chile | 0.50 | 21 980 | 10.0 | -- | 0.36 | 48 | 24.0 | 19.0 |

*Sources*: OECD (2015a, 2016a, 2016b, 2016c, 2016c, 2016d, 2016e); World Bank Group (2016)

**Policy Considerations for Limiting Inequality and Promoting Prosperity**

Let us now examine how differences in policy initiatives among OECD countries influence inequality and economic prosperity. Without question, social spending, which involves transfers to low- and middle-income earners, reduces income inequality. Such transfers compensate for high levels of market income inequality by taxing the rich and redistributing income to the poor. However, this chapter focuses largely on the impact of policies that influence market income inequality. While such policies typically require extensive tax revenue to fund them, they do not directly redistribute incomes through transfers. The policies we will consider fall under two general headings: making education and labour markets more efficient; and maintaining and attracting businesses.

EDUCATION AND LABOUR MARKET EFFICIENCY. In Canada, there exists little coordination between government, employers and labour to help ensure a match between labour force skills and the needs of the economy. This lack of coordination has resulted in an overemphasis on general university education with little consideration

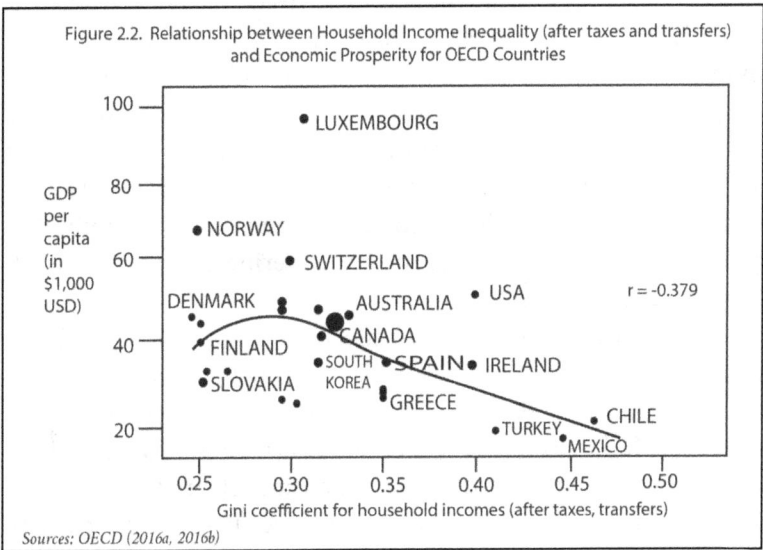

Figure 2.2. Relationship between Household Income Inequality (after taxes and transfers) and Economic Prosperity for OECD Countries

Sources: OECD (2016a, 2016b)

for job-specific training. Thus, while Canada has one of the most highly educated workforces in the world—58 percent of the 25–35 age cohort has a tertiary education (OECD, 2015)—employees often lack the skills required by employers. Experience from other countries suggests that such high levels of tertiary education are not necessary or even desirable for ensuring high productivity. The educational profile of European populations looks radically different (OECD, 2015a). For example, many countries with levels of GDP per capita comparable to Canada's but with much lower levels of income inequality have a much lower percentage of the population obtaining tertiary qualifications (41.2 percent in Denmark, 46.6 percent in Norway, 42.9 percent in the Netherlands, and 29.9 percent in Germany).

In contrast to Canada and the USA, many European countries also tend to be characterized by a high level of labour market coordination. That is, labour relations are negotiated in a tripartite system of employees' organizations, employers' representatives and government (Soskice, 1994). Although largely focused on employees' wages and benefits, such negotiations also consider the needs of the economy and how labour and government can ensure those needs are met. Important in this regard is the type of training that employers are looking for in their employees; employers influence education policy so it attends to their needs (Iversen & Soskice, 2001; Estevez-Abe, Iversen & Soskice, 2001). Such coordination improves the match between education and occupational outcomes, thus lowering inequality (Andersen & Van de Werfhorst, 2010). In addition, coordination has led to low corporate taxes and high consumption taxes, which enable governments to gain consent for high individual income taxes and social programs that protect low-income earners, further lowering inequality (Hall & Soskice, 2001; Martin, 2015).

Two recent developments affecting Canadian universities demonstrate the comparative lack of insight Canadian governments have with respect to how educational policy affects the economy. Influenced by the federal government, provincial governments have promoted a vast expansion of graduate training in Canadian universities over the past decade or so. Faced with serious funding constraints, most universities have been forced to accept government incentives to increase the number of graduate programs and graduate students. However, the market does not require the increased number of PhDs that the universities are producing. The problem is complicated by the end of mandatory retirement at age 65. It is not unusual for tenured professors to remain employed full-time into their 70s, even though they are often required to receive full salaries and full pension benefits at the same time (Brym, 2015). Thus, the number of PhDs has swollen precisely when the number of positions for these people has shrunk. Coordination among groups representing employers, employees and government could have prevented this problem.

Evidence also suggests that the match between education and occupational outcomes is strongest in "dual" education systems characterized by strong vocational specificity and extensive tracking of students at the secondary level (Allmendinger, 1989; Brauns et al., 1999; Kerckhoff, 2001; Shavit & Müller, 1998; Scherer, 2005). Vocational specificity refers to the amount of institutionalized apprenticeship training that combines work experience with schooling designed to improve occupation-specific skills (Kerckhoff 2001). Secondary-level tracking controls access to tertiary education by placing students in tertiary or vocational streams. Such systems provide clear signals of potential employees' qualifications, making it easier for employers to hire personnel with required skills. As a result, people are more likely to find suitable employment soon after graduation and less likely be underemployed than would otherwise be the case (Breen 2005; Shavit & Müller 1998; Van der Velden & Wolbers, 2003). For the labour market as a whole, the match between education and occupation tends to be strongest in dual systems, and even more so for those with vocational training (Scherer 2005). Combining such a system with labour market coordination ensures that the training needs of both individuals and business are met. The typical result is a society characterized by a relatively small proportion of the labour force with university degrees and a relatively large proportion of the labour force with job skills needed by the economy. These circumstances simultaneously increase productivity and lower income inequality.

MAINTAINING AND ATTRACTING BUSINESS. Globalization has made it easy for corporations to leave Canada. In fact, the North American Free Trade Agreement (NAFTA) incentivizes them to do so. Setting aside differences in environmental regulations and labour laws, the fact that the average Mexican wage is 27 percent lower than the average Canadian wage is probably enough reason for companies to leave Canada under conditions that allow free movement of capital (OECD, 2015b). As corporations leave, so do jobs, contributing to the rise in income inequality. Because free trade is unlikely to end anytime soon, we are left with the question of what can be done to keep businesses in Canada.

To avoid plant closures, labour has often had to make concessions to business, such as accepting wage freezes or even wage reductions. However, another, European approach can more effectively entice businesses to remain in Canada. It involves lowering the non-wage costs of doing business by means of reforming corporate tax and employment regulation policies.

Often, people on the left of the political spectrum argue that jobs must be protected—without giving serious consideration to the negative impact this would have on business. While such protection might guarantee employment for people with jobs, it does not guarantee that jobs will exist. As trade borders weaken, capital—especially capital invested in manufacturing—becomes more mobile. From the point of view of profitability, it makes little sense for a company to manufacture products in a place characterized by high wages, high taxes and extensive regulation when it can move to locations that have significantly lower costs.

Although it might seem counterintuitive, making conditions better for business is part of the solution to decreasing the economic inequality that results from increased capital mobility. In particular, a move towards "flexicurity," a social welfare model first developed in Denmark, could pave the way.

The Danish flexicurity model rests on three pillars: (1) low employment protection for workers within firms; (2) a strong safety net for the unemployed; and (3) active labour market policies that facilitate re-employment of the unemployed. These principles allow business to be competitive in the global market while protecting workers. While low employment protection means that it is relatively easy for firms to lay off workers, extensive state policies facilitate finding new employment for displaced workers and ensure that they maintain a decent standard of living in the meantime. In addition, active labour policies provide incentives for displaced workers to get retrained and find new employment

(Bredgaard et al., 2005). Thus, Denmark's low economic inequality has been achieved by combining high levels of labour market flexibility and social security (Ebralidze, 2012: 160).

Although Danish employees enjoy much stronger protection from unfair dismissal than do their Canadian counterparts, Denmark's employers typically enjoy shorter notice periods, lower average severance payments, and far fewer procedural inconveniences for *collective* dismissals. For example, Danish firms with more than 100 employees need to give only 30 days' notice of a large collective dismissal, and firms with fewer than 20 employees are not required by law to give any notice (OECD, 2013: 20–21). On the other hand, Canadian firms must give 8 to 16 weeks' notice of a collective dismissal, depending on the province, number of employees, and number of employees to be dismissed (OECD, 2013: 12–13). Still, comparatively easy collective dismissal of Danish employees is countered by much more extensive employment insurance and social assistance. In 2014, unemployed Danish workers received 90 percent of their previous weekly income up to a maximum of DKK 3,940 (approximately CAD 756) per week for 104 weeks (OECD, 2016g); their Canadian counterparts were entitled to 55 percent of their previous income up to a maximum of CAD 514 per week for 45 weeks (OECD, 2016f). Significantly, however, the Danish system has stricter conditions for receiving such support. Unemployed workers expecting to receive unemployment insurance must participate in job counselling and assessment programs, undertake job retraining, and be willing to take wage-subsidized jobs. The level of such labour-force activation increases with duration of unemployment. As Table 2.1 indicates, in 2015, public expenditures on labour policies in Denmark amounted to 3.5 percent of GDP. In Canada, the comparable figure was 0.8 percent.

Flexicurity is only part of the Danish solution to job protection. In addition, corporate taxes are lower in Denmark than in most capitalist democracies (22 percent, compared to up to 31 percent in Canada and up to 47 percent in the USA; see Table 2.1). Low corporate taxes make it attractive for firms to do business in Denmark despite its high wages and extensive welfare state. As well as inducing companies to do business in Canada, reducing corporate taxes would make a significant increase in the minimum wage financially viable, even for small firms. An increase in the minimum wage would, in turn, contribute to wage compression—resulting in a decrease in income inequality—by increasing incomes at the bottom of the income distribution.

Market inequality will never disappear entirely, so an extensive welfare state will always be needed if the goal is to limit inequality. This fact begs the question of how the state can afford social spending, including extensive active labour market policies, if corporate taxes are low. The answer: generate more tax revenue from individuals instead of businesses. While most discussion on this issue usually revolves around redistributing incomes from the rich to the poor through progressive income taxes, other taxes are also effective. Although inherently regressive, consumption taxes (like the HST in Canada) are important for funding an extensive welfare state. As Table 2.1 indicates, high consumption taxes are a common feature of most OECD countries that enjoy relatively low income inequality. In social democratic welfare states, then, it is largely members of the middle class who pay for the welfare state from which they benefit (Korpi & Palme, 1998).

MULTIVARIATE MODELS. Table 2.2 offers an empirical test of the foregoing arguments. For the 34 OECD countries, it lists robust correlation coefficients and standardized robust regression coefficients predicting GDP per capita and the Gini coefficient for household incomes from the policy indicators discussed earlier. The regression coefficients were derived from models that control for all other policy variables.[1] The results in the top panel of Table 2.2 lend strong support to the idea that policies that benefit both business and individuals reduce inequality and increase prosperity. It is clear, for example, that economic prosperity is not negatively affected by social spending. The opposite appears to be true: a statistically significant positive correlation exists between social spending and GDP per capita. It is also clear that active labour policies and pro-business policies have a positive impact on

1. Given the small number of countries observed, robust estimates (MM-estimates) are employed to ensure that the estimated relationships are not unduly influenced by a small number of unusual countries (Andersen, 2008).

GDP per capita. This relationship holds both for the bivariate correlation and when controlling for other policy indicators. On the other hand, GDP per capita has no statistically significant effect on free tuition for tertiary education and the level of corporate or sales taxes. We can reasonably conclude that policies formulated to make business easier have a significant impact on prosperity.

The bottom panel of Table 2.2 indicates how these policies influence income inequality. A strong negative relationship exists between level of social spending and level of income inequality. This association reflects the importance of social spending in compensating for high inequality in market-generated incomes. In terms of how spending is allocated, education is one area of importance. Countries with free tertiary education tend to be more equal than countries without free tuition. Other factors also matter. Active labour market and pro-business policies have a negative impact on inequality. In contrast, corporate taxes have a positive effect on inequality. Put another way, incomes tend to be more equal in countries that make it attractive for business to operate. Without controls, less inequality is significantly associated with higher consumption taxes. However, the relationship is not statistically significant when the influence of the other variables is controlled.[2]

Conclusion

High income inequality comes with steep costs for business, government and civil society. It is especially painful for those at the bottom of the income distribution. Nevertheless, income inequality in Canada is higher than it has been for many decades and higher than that of many other OECD countries. Many rich European countries, especially in Scandinavia, are more prosperous than Canada yet have far lower income inequality. This fact suggests that reducing inequality does not need to come at the cost of declining economic prosperity. In fact, among OECD countries, a negative relationship exists between income inequality and pros-

2. The discrepancy in results reflects the relatively small number of countries (n=26) used in the analysis and collinearity associated with the strong relationship that sales taxes has with active labour market policies (r=0.60), pro-business policies (r=0.489) and corporate tax rates (r=-0.478).

perity. In short, low inequality on its own is not bad for business.

Redistributive policies are important if the goal is to reduce market-generated income inequality. All modern states provide some level of income redistribution but this is not the only way to

Table 2.2. Relationship between Economic Prosperity (GDP per capita), Income Inequality (Gini coefficient for household incomes) and Various Policy Initiatives, OECD Countries

| | Social Spending (n=34) | Active Labour Policies (n=28) | Free Tertiary Tuition (n=26) | Pro-Business Policies[b] (n=34) | Corporate Taxes (n=34) | Sales Taxes (n=34) |
|---|---|---|---|---|---|---|
| **GDP per capita** | | | | | | |
| Robust Correlation (MM-estimate) | 0.302** | 0.472** | -0.192 | 0.432*** | 0.071 | -0.114 |
| Robust Regression[a] (standardized MM-estimates) | -- | 0.642*** | -0.211 | 0.478*** | 0.440** | 0.028 |
| **Gini Coefficient (household incomes)** | | | | | | |
| Robust Correlation (MM-estimate) | - 0.568*** | -0.368** | - 0.491*** | -0.243* | 0.200* | -0.296** |
| Robust Regression[a] (standardized MM-estimates) | -- | -0.319* | - 0.417*** | 0.193* | 0.371** | 0.264 |

[a] Robust regression models predict GDP per capita and Gini coefficient from all policy initiative measures except social spending.
[b] This variable is measured as a rank, with low values indicating a high rank on the 'ease of doing business' measure (see Table 2.1). The variable was transformed before the making the calculations above by multiplying by -1 so that high values indicate pro-business.
***$p$-value<0.01; **$p$-value<0.05; *$p$-value<0.1

reduce inequality. OECD countries with the lowest level of income inequality tend to do much more. Denmark serves as a model in this regard. Although it is the most equal country in the world, it is also considered the best country in which to do business (Forbes, 2015). Danish governments have accomplished this feat by crafting educational and labour market policies that make it easy for companies to do business but simultaneously protect workers from unemployment and low wages. Particularly important is the Danish system of flexicurity, which gives employers flexibility in terms of how they employ their workforce, retrains displaced workers, helps them find new employment, and provides extensive social security in the event that they have trouble re-entering the employed labour force.

Flexicurity would be difficult to institute without extensive labour market coordination. In such systems, labour unions, employer groups and government come together to negotiate the needs of the economy. Such collaboration increases the chance that the labour force obtains the type and level of training required by employers. In other words, it ensures that the education system responds to the needs of the economy. Such coordination also typically results in extensive vocational components being grafted on to education systems, which further ensures appropriate training. Transparent qualifications make it easier for employers to hire the right personnel and for potential employees to find work that matches their skills. The final result, assuming proper planning, is a reduction in inequality that is produced by a poor match between training and jobs.

Introducing a new system for labour market coordination in Canada is a lofty and perhaps unrealistic goal. Countries characterized by such arrangements have long histories of coalitions between parties with different political interests (Esping-Andersen, 1993). The institutional arrangements required to create the system of flexicurity in Denmark, for example, have been well established for nearly a century. The more equal countries of the OECD also tend to have much stronger labour movements and union coverage than does Canada. It is also important to note that in terms of social policy, Canada is much more decentralized than most OECD countries (Obinger, Castels & Leibfried, 2005), with many policies coming under the jurisdiction of provincial governments. These are not simple obstacles to overcome, so it would be unrealistic to assume that extensive labour market coordination and a system of flexicurity could develop quickly in Canada. This does not mean that Canada could not take steps toward better coordination, however. In fact, Quebec has done so (Haddow, 2015). At the very least, more consultation would help Canadian governments better understand how to make better investments in public education.

It seems likely that some of the pro-business policies discussed in this chapter could easily be implemented even without greater labour market coordination but even these would require some sort of deal making. While it is unlikely that the working and middle classes will see the benefit of reducing corporate taxes and increasing consumption taxes in the present political climate, they may be more open to the idea if it were obvious that companies were more likely to do business in Canada as a result. However, having companies stay in Canada likely would not be enough. Assurances would have to exist that workers would receive other benefits too, such as an increase in the minimum wage and extensive government-funded training in the event that they become unemployed.

In conclusion, the analysis presented here suggests that the best strategy to reduce income inequality in Canada would involve consideration of the conditions that make business as easy as possible and at the same ensure a high level of employment security for workers. The journey would not be easy. It would involve business, labour and government working together to achieve the common goals of greater prosperity and equality, which, it should now be clear, are not incommensurable.

## References

Allmendinger, Jutta. 1989. 'Educational Systems and Labour Market Outcomes,' *European Sociological Review*, 5: 231–50.

Andersen, Robert. 2008. Modern Methods for Robust Regression. Sage University Paper series on Quantitative Applications in the Social Sciences, 07-152. Thousand Oaks, CA: Sage.

Andersen, Robert. 2012. 'Support for Democracy in Cross-national Perspective: The Detrimental Effect of Economic Inequality,' *Research in Social Stratification and Mobility*, 30(4): 389–402.

Andersen, Robert & Tina Fetner. 2008. 'Economic Inequality and Intolerance: Attitudes toward Homosexuality in 35 Democracies,' *American Journal of Political Science*, 52 (4):942-958.

Andersen, Robert & Mitch McIvor. 2014. 'Rising Inequality and Its Impact in Canada: The Role of National Debt', In *Changing Inequalities and Societal Impacts in Thirty Rich Countries: Thirty Countries' Experiences*, edited by Brian Nolan, Wiemer Salverda, Daniele Checchi, Ive Marx, Abigail McKnight, István György Tóth & Herman van de Werfhorst. Oxford: Oxford University Press.

Andersen, Robert & Herman van de Werfhorst. 2010. 'Education and Occupational Status in 14 Countries: The Role of Educational Institutions and Labour Market Coordination,' *British Journal of Sociology*, 61(2): 336-355.

Battle, Ken, Michael Mendelson & Sherri Torjman. 2005. 'The Modernization Mantra: Toward a New Architecture for Canada's Adult Benefits,' *Canadian Public Policy/Analyse de Politiques* 31: 431-7.

Banting, Keith. 2005. 'Canada: Nation-Building in a Federal Welfare State,' In Herbert Obinger, Stephan Leibfried and Frank G. Castles, eds., *Federalism and the Welfare State: New World and European Experiences*. Cambridge: Cambridge University Press, pp. 89–137.

Banting, Keith G. 2006. 'Dis-embedding Liberalism? The New Social Policy Paradigm in Canada,' In *Dimensions of Inequality in Canada*, ed. David A. Green and Jonathan R. Kesselman. Vancouver: UBC Press, pp. 417–52.

Bebchuck, Lucien A., Martijn Cremers & Urs Peyer. 2011. 'The CEO Pay Slice,' *Journal of Financial Economics*, 102: 199–221.

Brauns, H., Steinmann, S., Kieffer, A. & Marry, C. 1999. 'Does Education Matter? France and Germany in Comparative Perspective,' *European Sociological Review*, 15: 61–90.

Bredgaard, T., F. Larsen & P.K. Madsen. 2005. 'The Flexible Danish Labour Market: A Review,' CARMA Research Paper 1, Centre for Labour Market Research (CARMA), University of Aalborg.

Breen, Richard. 2005. 'Explaining Cross-national Variation in Youth Unemployment: Market and Institutional Factors,' *European Sociological Review* 21: 125–34.

Brym, Robert. 2015. 'How Ontario dropped the ball on mandatory retirement,' iPolitics.ca. 27 February. http://projects.chass.utoronto.ca/brym/retirement.pdf.

Card, David & John E. DiNardo. 2002. "Skill-Biased Technological Change and Rising Wage Inequality: Some Problems and Puzzles." *Journal of Labor Economics*, 20 (4):733–783.

Cranford, Cynthia J., Leah F. Vosko & Nancy Zukewich. 2003. 'Precarious Employment in the Canadian Labour Market: A Statistical Portrait,' *Just Labour* 3: 6–22.

Ebralidze, Ellen. 2012. Rising employment flexibility and young workers' economic insecurity. A comparative analysis of the Danish model of flexicurity. Farmington Hills, MI: Budrich UniPress.

Esping-Andersen, Gøsta. 1993. *Changing Classes: Stratification and Mobility in Post-Industrial Societies*. Sage Studies in International Sociology, Sage Publications, Ltd.

Estevez-Abe, M., Iversen, T. & Soskice, D. 2001. 'Social Protection and the Formation of Skills: A Reinterpretation of the Welfare State,' In P.A. Halland D. Soskice (eds.) *Varieties of Capitalism. The Institutional Foundations of Comparative Advantage*. Oxford: Oxford University Press.

Ferris, J. Stephen & Stanley L. Winer. 2007. 'Just How Much Bigger is Government in Canada? A Comparative Analysis of the Size and Structure of the Public Sectors in Canada and the United States, 1929–2004." *Canadian Public Policy – Analyse De Politiques*, 33(2): 173–206.

Finnie, Ross & Ian Irvine. 2011. 'The Redistributional Impact of Canada's Employment Insurance Program,' *Canadian Public Policy* 37(2): 201–218.

Forbes. 2016. Best Countries for Business. http://www.forbes.com/best-countries-for-business/list/#tab:overall.

Fortin, Nicole, David A. Green, Thomas Lemieux, Kevin Milligan & W. Craig Riddell. 2012. 'Canadian Inequality: Recent Developments and Policy Options.' *Canadian Public Policy*, 38(2): 121–145.

Frenette, Marc, David A. Green & Kevin Milligan. 2009. 'Taxes, Transfers, and

Canadian Income Inequality,'" *Canadian Public Policy/Analyse de Politiques* 35: 389–411.

Gelinas, Patrice & Lisa Baillargeon. 2013. "CEO Compensation in Canada, 1971–2008." *International Journal of Business and Management* 8(12): 1–7.

Golden, Miriam and Michael Wallerstein. 2006. 'Domestic and International Causes for the Rise of Pay Inequality: Post-Industrialism, Globalization and Labour Market Institutions,' Working Paper 2010–08; Institute for Research on Labor and Employment. University of California, Los Angeles

Grabb, Edward, Robert Andersen, Monica Hwang & Scott Milligan. 2009. 'Confidence in Political Institutions in Canada and the United States: Assessing the Interactive Role of Region and Race,' *American Review of Canadian Studies*, 39(4): 379–397.

Greenspon, Edward & Anthony Wilson-Smith. 1996. *Double Vision: The Inside Story of the Liberals in Power*. Toronto: Doubleday Canada.

Haddow, Rodney. 2015. *Comparing Quebec and Ontario: Political Economy and Public Policy at the Turn of the Millennium*. Toronto: University of Toronto Press.

Hall, P.A. & Soskice, D. 2001. *Varieties of Capitalism. The Institutional Foundations of Comparative Advantage*. Oxford: Oxford University Press.

Heisz, Andrew. 2007. 'Income Inequality and Redistribution in Canada: 1976 to 2004,' Analytical Studies Branch Research Paper Series. Ottawa: Statistics Canada.

Hou, Feng & John Myles. 2008. 'The changing role of education in the marriage market: assertive marriage in Canada & the United States since the 1970s,'. *Canadian Journal of Sociology* 33:337–366.

Iversen, T. & Soskice, D. 2001 'An Asset Theory of Social Policy Preferences', *American Political Science Review* 95: 875– 93.

Korpi, Walter & Joakim Palme. 1998. 'The Paradox of Redistribution and Strategies of Equality: Welfare State Institutions, Inequality, and Poverty in the Western Countries,' *American Sociological Review* 63 (5): 661–687.

Johnson, George. 1997. "Changes in Earnings Inequality: The Role of Demand Shifts." *Journal of Economic Perspectives*, 11: 41–54.

Jorgenson, Dale W. 2001. "Information Technology and the U. S. Economy." *American Economic Review* 91 (March): 1–32.

Katz, Lawrence. 1999. "Technological Change, Computerization, and the Wage Structure." Unpublished manuscript. Cambridge, MA: Harvard University, Department of Economics.

Kenworthy, L. 2001 'Wage-Setting Measures: A Survey and Assessment', *World Politics* 54: 57–98.

Kerckhoff, A.C. 2001 'Education and Social Stratification Processes in Comparative Perspective', *Sociology of Education*, 74: 3–18.

Martin, Cathie Jo. 2015. 'Labour market coordination and the evolution of tax regimes,' *Socioeconomic Review*: 13(1):33–54.

Milligan, Scott, Robert Andersen & Robert Brym. 2014. 'Assessing Variation in Tolerance in 23 Muslim-Majority and Western Countries,' *Canadian Review of*

*Sociology*, 51: (3): 239–261.

Minister of Finance. 2006. Canada's New Government Cuts Wasteful Programs, Refocuses Spending on Priorities, Achieves Major Debt Reduction as Promised. Ottawa: Finance.

Myles, John. 1998. 'How to Design a 'Liberal' Welfare State: A Comparison of Canada and the United States,' *Social Policy and Administration* 32(4): 341–364.

Obinger, H., S. Leibfried & F. G. Castles (eds.). 2005. *Federalism and the Welfare State: New World and European Experiences*. Cambridge: Cambridge University Press.

Osberg, Lars and Pierre Fortin. 1998. *Hard Money, Hard Times: Why Zero Inflation Hurts Canadians*. Toronto, ON: James Lorimer & Company Publishers.

OECD. 2013. Detailed Description of Employment Protection Legislation, 2012–2014 OECD Countries. http://www.oecd.org/els/emp/All.pdf.

OECD. 2015a. Education at a Glance 2015: OECD Indicators, OECD Publishing, Paris. http://dx.doi.org/10.1787/eag-2015-en.

OECD. 2015b. OECD Employment Outlook 2015, OECD Publishing, Paris. http://dx.doi.org/10.1787/empl_outlook-2015-en.

OECD. 2016a. Income Distribution Database (IDD): Gini, poverty, income, methods and concepts. http://www.oecd.org/social/income-distribution-database.htm.

OECD. 2016b. Gross domestic product (GDP) (indicator). http://10.1787/dc2f7aec-en.

OECD. 2016c. Social Expenditure Database (SOCX), http://www.oecd.org/social/expenditure.htm.

OECD. 2016d. Public spending on labour markets (indicator). DOI: 10.1787/911b8753-en.

OECD. 2016e. 'Revenue Statistics: Comparative tables,' OECD Tax Statistics (database).http://dx.doi.org/10.1787/data-00262-en.

OECD. 2016f. Benefits and Wages: Country specific information (Canada). http://www.oecd.org/els/soc/benefits-and-wages-country-specific-information.htm.

OECD. 2016g. Benefits and Wages: Country specific information (Denmark). http://www.oecd.org/els/soc/benefits-and-wages-country-specific-information.htm.

Pablo A. Mitnik, Erin Cumberworth & David B. Grusky. 2012. Social Mobility in a High Inequality Regime. Unpublished paper, June 2012. Stanford Center on Poverty and Inequality 450 Serra Mall, Bldg. 370 Stanford University Stanford, CA 94305.

Picot, Garnett & John Myles. 1995. 'Social Transfers, Changing Family Structure, and Low Income Among Children,' Statistics Canada Working Paper No. 82. http://ssrn.com/abstract=3202 or http://dx.doi.org/10.2139/ssrn.3202.

Saez, Emmanuel & Veall, Michael R. 2003. 'The Evolution of High Incomes in Canada, 1920– 2000,' National Bureau of Economic Research, Inc., NBER Working Papers: No. 9607, 2003.

Saez, E. & M. Veall. 2005. 'The Evolution of High Incomes in Northern America: Lessons from Canadian Evidence,'" *American Economic Review* 95 (3): 831–49.

Shavit, Y. & Müller, W. 1998. *From School to Work. A Comparative Study of Educational*

*Qualifications and Occupational Destinations.* Oxford: Clarendon Press.

Scherer, S. 2005. 'Patterns of Labour Market Entry: Long Wait or Career Instability? An Empirical Comparison of Italy, Great Britain and West Germany', *European Sociological Review* 21: 427–40.

Soskice, David. 1994 'Reconciling Markets and Institutions: The German Apprenticeship System' in L. M. Lynch (ed.) *Training and the Private Sector: International Comparisons.* Chicago: University of Chicago Press.

Statistics Canada. 2016. Table 206-0033: Gini coefficients of adjusted market, total and after-tax income, Canada and provinces, annual, CANSIM (database).

Stiglitz, Joseph E. 2012. *The Price of Inequality: How Today's Divided Society Endangers Our Future.* New York: W.W. Norton & Company

Stiglitz, Joseph E. 2015. *The Great Divide: Unequal Societies and What We Can Do about Them.* New York: W.W. Norton & Company.

Tupper, Allan. 1993. 'Think Tanks, Public Debt and the Politics of Expertise in Canada,' *Canadian Public Administration,* 36, 4: 530–46.

Uslaner, Eric M. 2002. *The Moral Foundations of Trust.* Cambridge: Cambridge University Press.

Uslaner, Eric M. & Mitchell Brown. 2005. 'Inequality, Trust, and Civic Engagement.' *American Politics Research* 33(6): 868–94.

Van der Velden, R.K.W. & Wolbers, M.H.J. 2003. 'The Integration of Young People into the Labour Market: The Role of Training Systems and Labour Market Regulation', in W. Müller and M. Gangl (eds.) *Transitions from Education to Work in Europe. The Integration of Youth into EU Labour Markets.* Oxford: Oxford University Press.

Visser, Jelle, Sabina Avdagic & Martin Rhodes (eds.). 2011. *Social Pacts in Europe. Emergence, Evolution and Institutionalization.* Oxford: Oxford University Press.

Vosko, Leah F. 2006. *Precarious Employment: Understanding Labour Market Insecurity in Canada.* McGill-Queen's University Press.

World Bank Group. 2016. Doing Business. Measuring Business Regulations. http://www.doingbusiness.org/rankings.

# CHAPTER THREE

# How Much Can Income Tax on the Top 1 Percent Be Raised?

## Lars Osberg

### Introduction

Over the last 35 years, Canada has seen substantial increases in market income at the top of the income distribution while middle-class incomes have stagnated (Osberg: 2008a, 2014). Simultaneously, top income tax rates have declined significantly. An increasing fraction of Canada's total potential tax base has thus become concentrated at the top but is now taxed at a lower marginal rate. At the same time, cuts to social programs and public services have undermined the well-being of less well-off Canadians—cuts that could have been less severe or even avoided if Canadians with the greatest ability to pay taxes had not received tax rate reductions.

Top tax rates are therefore increasingly important for both government budgets and the fairness of the distribution of disposable income, which has motivated a surge of research on how much income tax the top 1 percent could and should pay. The International Monetary Fund (2013) has estimated that Canada's current top income tax rate has been well below the revenue-maximizing tax rate and the top marginal income tax rate in Canadian provinces has been relatively low compared both to most other OECD nations and to most US states. Moreover, the tax rates paid by Canada's top income tax filers have been considerably less than nominal top marginal rates.

So how much more could Canada's top 1 percent be paying in taxes? I argue that the standard methodology used to calculate the revenue maximizing top marginal income tax rate underestimates the optimal top tax rate. In this chapter, I also summarize evidence on possible migration responses to top-end tax differentials, discuss the policy room available for sub-national governments, and address the quiet side of tax policy: avoidance and evasion. I conclude that there is room for a significant increase in the top marginal income tax rate in Canada. Specifically, with an effective top marginal tax rate of 65 percent, I calculate revenue gain between $15 billion and $19 billion for income excluding capital gains and $21.8 billion to $26.1 billion for income including capital gains.

Table 3.1. Income Growth and Top Percentile Share, 1975–2007 (in percent)

|  | Average annual real income growth | Top 1% annual real income growth | Bottom 99% annual real income growth | Fraction of total growth captured by top 1% |
|---|---|---|---|---|
| Canada | 0.7 | 2.65 | 0.5 | 37.3 |
| United States | 1.0 | 3.9 | 0.6 | 46.9 |
| Denmark | 0.7 | 0.4 | 0.7 | 2.5 |
| France | 0.8 | 1.1 | 0.8 | 11.4 |
| New Zealand | 0.8 | 2.3 | 0.8 | 14.3 |
| Australia | 1.1 | 3.5 | 0.9 | 22.5 |
| Italy | 1.5 | 2.2 | 1.4 | 11.5 |
| Portugal | 1.5 | 1.2 | 1.5 | 7.5 |
| Sweden | 1.6 | 2.5 | 1.5 | 8.8 |
| United Kingdom | 1.9 | 4.5 | 1.6 | 24.3 |
| Spain | 2.0 | 2.4 | 1.9 | 10.1 |
| Norway | 2.4 | 5.6 | 2.3 | 11.7 |

Source: Förster, Llena-Nozal & Nafilyan (2014: 25).

Table 3.2. Top Marginal Tax Rates, 2015

| Province | Top Marginal Provincial Income Tax Rate |
|---|---|
| Newfoundland and Labrador | 14.3% on the amount over $175,000 |
| Prince Edward Island | 16.7% on the amount over $63,969 |
| Nova Scotia | 21% on the amount over $150,000 |
| New Brunswick | 17.84% on the amount over $129,975 |
| Quebec | 21% on the amount over $102,040 |
| Ontario | 20.53% (= 13.16 * 1.56 surtaxes) on the amount over $220,000 |
| Manitoba | 17.4% on the amount over $67,000 |
| Saskatchewan | 15% on the amount over $125,975 |
| Alberta | 10% of taxable income |
| British Columbia | 16.8% on the amount over $151,050 |

Source: Boat Harbour Investments (2016a); Canada Revenue Agency (2016).

As a point of reference, Figure 3.1 reproduces the International Monetary Fund's recent estimates of the revenue-maximizing top marginal income tax rate in 16 affluent countries. Canada has the fourth-lowest top marginal income tax rate, higher only than New Zealand, the Czech Republic and the United States. The International Monetary Fund concludes that Canada, like many other countries, has significant room for increasing top marginal tax rates. Their conclusions are not unusual. Atkinson (2014) has suggested a top tax rate of 65 percent, Diamond & Saez (2011) and Saez, Slemrod & Giertz (2012) argued for a 73 percent top tax rate, Piketty, Saez & Stantcheva, (2011) advocated 83 percent and Kindermann & Krueger (2014) suggested the top tax rate should be 90 percent.

Although some might argue that low tax rates for top income earners bring "trickle-down" benefits in faster income growth for those at the bottom of the income hierarchy, Table 3.1 dispels that notion. Among wealthy countries, the US and Canada have relatively low top tax rates. They also share the bottom two spots in international comparisons of the growth rate of the real pre-tax income of the bottom 99 percent of the population and the top two spots in international comparisons of the share of total income growth received by the top 1 percent.

## Top Marginal Income Tax Rates in Canada over Time

By historical standards, too, top income tax rates in Canada have been relatively low in recent years. As Figure 3.2 illustrates, the top marginal income tax rate has been well over 50 percent for most of the time that Canada has had an income tax system. The 1940 to 1980 period of significantly rising real incomes for the bottom 90 percent of the Canadian population was also a period when the top marginal income tax rate was well over 70 percent. Apart from a brief period in the 1920s, the years from 1982 to the present stand out as a time of exceptionally low top marginal tax rates.

From 2000 to 2015 in Canada, the federal government's top marginal income tax rate was stationary at 29 percent while the provinces had different add-on tax schedules in which the top tax rate kicked in at different levels of taxable income, as Table 3.2 shows. Since then, the new federal Liberal government has implemented a top federal income tax bracket (over $200,000) with a marginal rate of 33 percent. For 2016, Alberta also added brackets culminating in a 15 percent top tax rate over $300,000, New Brunswick proposed additional brackets with a top tax rate of 25.75 percent on income over $250,000, and Newfoundland also edged up to 15.3 percent on income over $175,000.

Top Tax Rates in Canadian Provinces and US States

In 2016, as Canada's new provincial and federal governments contemplated the fulfilment of their campaign promises, they encountered much rhetoric about the competition for talent and capital within North America and the dangers for economic growth of being a high tax jurisdiction. Table 3.3 therefore compares the total top 2013 marginal tax rate on labour income for each province and US state by adding federal and provincial/state income tax rates. The two highest top marginal tax rate jurisdictions in the US (New

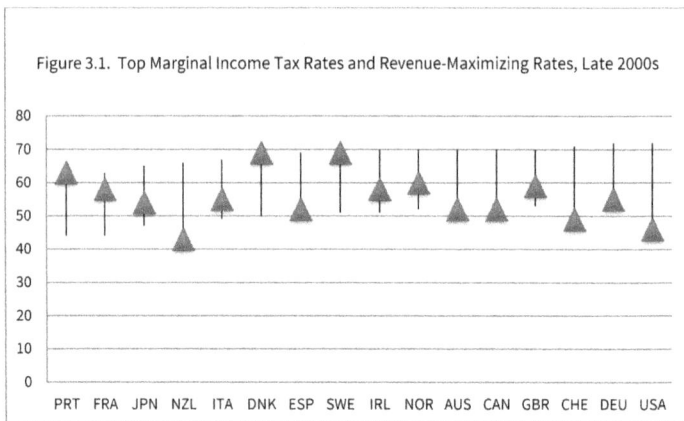

Figure 3.1. Top Marginal Income Tax Rates and Revenue-Maximizing Rates, Late 2000s

*Line indicates range of revenue-maximizing rates, triangle actual rate. Source: IMF (2016: 37).*

York City and California) include two of the most dynamic and high-income areas in the country, Wall Street and Silicon Valley. For high-income earners, the two lowest top marginal income tax rate jurisdictions in North America were both in Canada (Newfoundland and Alberta). On average, Canada was a low-tax jurisdiction for the affluent compared to the US. In 2013 the average US top marginal income tax rate (47.9 percent) was higher than the average Canadian rate (45.7 percent).

## Table 3.3. Top Marginal Tax Rate on Wage Income, 2013

| Rank | State/Province | Rate | Rank | State/Province | Rate |
|------|----------------|------|------|----------------|------|
| 1 | California | 51.9% | 32 | Massachusetts | 47.1% |
| 2 | Hawaii | 50.5% | 32 | Oklahoma | 47.1% |
| 3 | New York* | 50.3% | 34 | Illinois | 46.9% |
| 4 | Quebec | 50.0% | 34 | Kansas | 46.9% |
| 4 | Nova Scotia | 50.0% | 34 | Mississippi | 46.9% |
| 6 | Oregon | 49.9% | 34 | New Mexico | 46.9% |
| 7 | Minnesota | 49.8% | 34 | Utah | 46.9% |
| 8 | Ontario | 49.5% | 39 | Arizona | 46.7% |
| 9 | New Jersey | 49.3% | 39 | Colorado | 46.7% |
| 9 | Vermont | 49.3% | 39 | Indiana | 46.7% |
| 9 | Washington, D.C. | 49.3% | 39 | Pennsylvania | 46.7% |
| 12 | Maryland | 49.2% | 43 | Michigan | 46.6% |
| 13 | Maine | 49.0% | 44 | Manitoba | 46.4% |
| 14 | North Carolina | 48.6% | 45 | North Dakota | 46.3% |
| 14 | Wisconsin | 48.6% | 46 | Louisiana | 46.1% |
| 16 | Ohio | 48.5% | 47 | Alabama | 45.7% |
| 17 | Idaho | 48.4% | 48 | New Brunswick | 45.1% |
| 17 | Kentucky | 48.4% | 49 | Saskatchewan | 44.0% |
| 19 | Arkansas | 48.1% | 50 | British Columbia | 43.7% |
| 19 | Montana | 48.1% | 51 | Alaska | 42.8% |
| 19 | South Carolina | 48.1% | 51 | Florida | 42.8% |
| 22 | Delaware | 48.0% | 51 | Nevada | 42.8% |
| 22 | Nebraska | 48.0% | 51 | New Hampshire | 42.8% |
| 24 | Connecticut | 47.9% | 51 | South Dakota | 42.8% |
| 25 | West Virginia | 47.8% | 51 | Tennessee | 42.8% |
| 26 | Missouri | 47.6% | 51 | Texas | 42.8% |
| 27 | Georgia | 47.5% | 51 | Washington | 42.8% |
| 27 | Rhode Island | 47.5% | 51 | Wyoming | 42.8% |
| 29 | Iowa | 47.4% | 60 | Newfoundland | 42.3% |
| 29 | Virginia | 47.4% | 61 | Alberta | 39.0% |
| 29 | Prince Edward Island | 47.4% | Canada Average | | 45.7% |
| | | | US Average | | 47.9% |

* 51.7% in New York City. Sources: Figure 1; Table 2; Pomerlau (2014).

## Nominal and Actual Tax Rates at the Top

So far, the nominal top marginal income tax rate on labour income has been compared. However, Canadian tax law allows income of different types to be taxed at different rates. For example, in

Ontario in 2015, for taxpayers with taxable income in excess of $220,000, the combined federal and provincial top marginal income tax rate was 24.76 percent for capital gains income, 33.82 percent for eligible Canadian dividend income, and 40.13 percent for non-eligible Canadian dividend income. Only labour earnings and "other income" faced the combined federal and provincial top marginal income tax rate of 49.53 percent (Boat Harbour Investments, 2016b).

Table 3.4.  Average Income Tax Paid, 5-Year Averages, 2008–12

| Total Income | Top 0.01% | Top 0.1% | Top 1% | Top 5% | Top 10% | Top 50% |
|---|---|---|---|---|---|---|
| Average Income | 5,349,620 | 1,737,400 | 441,000 | 196,980 | 144,620 | 68,300 |
| Average Taxes* | 1,819,780 | 556,480 | 146,800 | 56,420 | 37,800 | 13,260 |
| Avg. % Tax Rate | 34.0% | 35.4% | 33.3% | 28.6% | 26.1% | 19.4% |
| Total Income with Capital Gains | Top 0.01% | Top 0.1% | Top 1% | Top 5% | Top 10% | Top 50% |
| Average Income | 6,267,080 | 1,827,120 | 494,980 | 211,660 | 152,760 | 70,320 |
| Average Taxes* | 1,847,880 | 554,900 | 146,720 | 56,520 | 37,860 | 13,280 |
| Avg. % Tax Rate | 29.5% | 30.4% | 29.6% | 26.7% | 24.8% | 18.9% |

*Average federal and provincial or territorial income taxes paid. Source: CANSIM (2015b).

As Table 3.4 indicates, the average income tax rate that is actually paid by top income earners is considerably lower than Table 3.3 would imply, even combining federal and provincial or territorial income tax. When the average tax rate is nearly constant, as it is

Figure 3.2.  Marginal Tax Rates in Canada for Various Percentiles

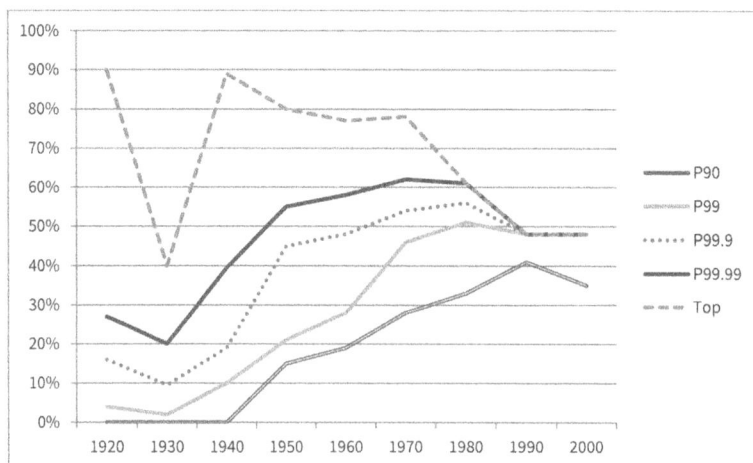

Source: Saez & Veall (2003: 90).

for the top 1 percent when capital gains are included, the marginal tax rate must equal the average rate (approximately 30 percent). If capital gains are excluded, comparing the increase in average total income tax paid when moving from roughly $200,000 to about $440,000 with the increase in income tax over the range $1.7 million to $5.3 million, the implied marginal income tax rate actually declines slightly (from 37.1 percent to 33.4 percent).

Evidently, there is a significant difference between nominal top marginal income tax rates on labour income and the tax rates actually paid. The estimates of Figure 3.1 and the typical recommendations that economists make regarding revenue-maximizing top marginal rates assume that taxpayers pay the stated nominal tax rate. Hence, the revenue and behavioural implications of implementing such tax rates are twofold: (1) the impact of moving from current actual tax rates to stated nominal rates (for the top 0.1 percent, an increase of roughly 10 percentage points, since the nominal average top rate in 2013 was 45.7 percent and the actual effective marginal tax rate paid was 35.4 percent, if capital gains are ignored) and (2) the impact of an increase in tax rates. For example, the 65 percent recommendation of Atkinson (2014) would suggest a further increase of about 19 percentage points in nominal rates, for a total increase of 29 percentage points.

### Tax Avoidance and Evasion: The Quiet Side of Tax Policy

Tax policy is only partly about nominal tax rates. Total tax yield also depends on the definitions of taxable income built into tax law (what some people call "loopholes") and the enforcement efforts of government. A low actual rate of income taxation can be achieved by specifying a low nominal tax rate or by building in tax avoidance mechanisms that are easily accessed through tax law or by tolerating low levels of compliance with tax law. As Förster, Llena-Nozal and Nafilyan (2014:59) note: "Tax avoidance . . . may be considered as a policy choice, since it may be reduced by limiting tax avoidance opportunities and improving tax enforcement." However, from the point of view of the affluent, a major advantage of public policy that facilitates tax avoidance or fails to penalize tax evasion is relative invisibility.

Changing the nominal tax rate may attract public attention and political debate. However, the complexity of tax law precludes much public discussion of the desirability of the tax law provisions that enable tax avoidance, while tax evasion is, by its nature, concealed. A few activists may raise objections, but they often struggle to gain public attention. Since the beneficiaries of quiet public policy decisions that enable tax avoidance or tolerate tax evasion have no reason to complain, and few other people know what is going on, there is little impetus for change.

In Canada, the tax treatment of Canadian Controlled Private Corporations (CCPCs) is an important case in point. Wolfson, Veall and Brooks (2014) note that for high-income individuals in Canada there can be major tax advantages in flowing income through a CCPC. Deferral of taxation, the potential to split income with family members in lower tax brackets and the potential to restructure income as capital gains can enable major tax savings. Although not usually an option for salaried employees, it is relatively inexpensive to incorporate and receive professional or business income through a CCPC—income that does not appear in the statistics on top-end incomes such as those reported in Table 3.4. Wolfson, Veall and Brooks (2014: 9) emphasize the complexity of CCPC structures and ownership and note that sophisticated tax planning often involves multiple layers of CCPCs. (There were about 1.95 million CCPCs in 2010, of which 1.7 million were traceable.) Fewer than 5 percent of tax filers in the bottom half of the income distribution owned shares in a CCPC (and these could be family members who are income splitting with top earners) but roughly 70 percent of tax filers among the top 0.01 percent own one or more CCPCs. In total, Wolfson Veall and Brooks (2014) estimate CCPC income in 2010 at $48 billion, which is about 44 percent of the total declared income of the top 1 percent of tax filers in that year. Their lower-bound estimate is that "when CCPC income is added, the share of the top 1 percent rises by 3.3 percentage points to 13.3%." And they note that "for the top 1%, taking account of CCPC income adds over $100,000, CCPC income adds more than $600,000 for the top 0.1%, and it adds from $2.7 to $3.5 million to measured annual income for the top 0.01%" (Wolfson, Veall & Brooks, 2014: 13).

As Table 3.4 indicates, there are currently huge tax advantages in Canada for receiving income in the form of capital gains and little public awareness or debate over why this might be socially desirable rather than mainly functioning as a benefit to Canadians with the most sophisticated tax advisors. Wolfson, Veall and Brooks (2014) have been shedding light on the importance of CCPCs but there is no comparable work available on the magnitude of the income sheltered in trust accounts or diverted to offshore banks and financial holding companies. Consequently, there is little reliable information on the full extent of tax avoidance and evasion in Canada.

However, it is clear that since the federal government, through the Canada Revenue Agency, administers the definition of the taxable income base and the collection of income taxes, it in turn is responsible for making daily administrative decisions that can lighten the tax load of affluent taxpayers. The federal government also defines the tax code and the regulations that can either impede or facilitate tax avoidance—including the banking regulations that either do or do not effectively monitor the offshore transfer of funds.

"Whistleblower rewards" are an example of the policy choices about tax collection quietly made by Canada's federal government. Tax evasion on a small scale can be a cash affair. Carpenters and electricians who work off the books can hide their undeclared cash in the garage and spend it on groceries—nobody else need know what they are doing. Tax evasion by the top 1 percent is different. Holding large sums as cash means forgoing any return on the capital and encountering adverse attention when making large cash purchases—but acquiring financial assets or real property leaves a paper trail. Indeed, some sort of paper trail is essential if the tax evader is to be sure of someday being able to get hidden money back. As a result, concealing serious money requires the cooperation of lawyers, accountants and bankers (and their secretaries and clerks). In the US, rewards to tax whistleblowers are a legal entitlement if the amounts in dispute exceed USD 2 million. Because the IRS pays whistleblowers 15 to 30 percent of the amount collected, the payout can be substantial—to date, the maximum whistleblower reward has been $104 million (Kocieniewski, 2012). In contrast, the Canada Revenue Agency website states primly: "The CRA does not in general pay for information received from informants" (Canada Revenue Agency, 2015; Internal Revenue Service, 2016). Large-scale tax evaders are the beneficiaries.

Top Tax Rates and Labour Supply

To estimate the revenue-maximizing top marginal income tax rate, the "standard" economics methodology (used by Piketty, Saez and Santcheva (2011, 2014), Milligan and Smart (2013, 2014), the International Monetary Fund and others) asks what size of work-effort change one can expect if top tax rates increase. An increase in the income tax rate will decrease the after-tax net hourly wage. The empirical issue is whether a decrease in the after-tax hourly wage causes a small or a large change in work effort. The key economic concept is the "after-tax wage elasticity of labour supply," which is defined as the percentage change in hours of work caused by a 1 percent change in the after-tax hourly wage. If the percentage change in work hours is assumed to be large, then an increase in the tax rate (that is, a decrease in the after-tax hourly wage) causes a large decrease in labour supply, which may be so large as to reduce total tax revenue. However, if the after-tax wage elasticity of labour supply is, for example, assumed to be 0.2 then even a 50 percent cut in the after-tax wage rate from raising the income tax rate will only have a 10 percent impact on work hours (since 50% * 0.2 = 10%), which means that tax revenue will increase. The crucial issue is whether the responsiveness of labour supply to higher tax rates has been overestimated and, as a consequence, whether the revenue-maximizing tax rates presented in Figure 1 are underestimates.

Taking the Total Time Constraint Seriously

Could "working harder" explain why the top 1 percent have higher incomes? Would they work less hard if the top tax rate was raised? If high incomes really are caused by greater labour supply, then lower income tax rates, which increase the net after-tax hourly wage, might cause an increase in labour supply by increasing the incentive to work more hours. However, how much could people work? A 16-hour a day workday, 365 days a year would imply 5,840 total annual hours, but this leaves no allowance for any interruption. If one day a week is allowed for rest, and if one day of annual holiday is taken, then annual work days would be 312, so working 16 hours a day on every workday implies annual working hours would be 16*312 = 4,992 hours. Many people might think this would be a pretty grim life, but at least total annual hours have an upper bound that is fairly easy to think about. In round numbers, an upper bound of roughly 5,000 work hours per year implies that a full-time, full-year, 2,000-hour per year worker (40 hours per week for 50 weeks per year) could possibly increase work hours by roughly 150 percent but no more.

To explain higher incomes by longer working hours one must face the fact that there only are 24 hours in a day and the range of hourly wages is many times greater than the possible range of work hours. Mackenzie (2015: 6) reports that, in 2013, the average annual compensation of Canada's top 100 CEOs was $9.2 million. On an hourly basis, if Canada's top CEOs worked 5,000 hours a year, their average hourly wage before tax would be $1,842. That wage is 7,894 percent of the median hourly wage of full-time employees in Canada in 2014 ($23.08). When hourly wages vary by so much more than working hours can possibly vary, it is clear that differences in working time can only explain a tiny part of the variation in top incomes.

Indeed, even within Canada's top 1 percent, one can ask: how much could differences in work effort possibly explain? In Canada in 2012, the range of top 1 percent incomes started at $213,800 in market income (not including capital gains) or $154,700 after tax. Assuming that one has to work full-year, full-time to make it into the top 1 percent, the 2,000 hours per year of work of the "threshold one percenter" implies an hourly after-tax wage of about $77. But the market income threshold for the top 0.01 percent ($2,605,900) was 1,219 percent greater (CANSIM, 2015b). Since the percentage range of incomes to be explained is so much greater than the feasible percentage change in work hours, each 1 percent increase in the net wage must necessarily have a tiny impact on work hours. Indeed, the greater the responsiveness of work effort to hourly wages one believes in, the faster work hours will approach the

5,000 hours maximum.[1]

Furthermore, as working hours approach total time available, the scarcity value of remaining leisure time increases, so it makes no sense for people to always increase hours of work in response to higher hourly net wages. Even very rich people need some non-work time in which to consume their income. Indeed, after some point further increases in the after-tax hourly wage may cause hours of work to decline, because when they get rich enough many people may decide that they can afford to enjoy more leisure.

When Piketty, Saez and Santcheva (2011, 2014) concluded that 83 percent is the revenue-maximizing top marginal income tax rate for the US, their key behavioural assumption was that the "effort elasticity" is 0.2 and that it remains constant over the entire range of top incomes. However, changed work effort is only one of the possible behavioural impacts of changing top marginal tax rates. High earners can also change their tax avoidance efforts and when tax rates decline it becomes more profitable for top corporate executives to bargain harder for higher pay at the expense of shareholders and other employees. Piketty, Saez and Santcheva (2011, 2014) argue that the strong negative correlation between top tax rates and top 1 percent income shares in the US since 1960 is mostly due to a reallocation of compensation from the bottom to the top.

Since more vigorous bargaining for higher CEO pay comes at the expense of other people's incomes—people who would pay taxes on that income if they could get it—the "bargaining elasticity" undercuts much of the argument against higher top marginal income tax rates. If higher top marginal income tax rates imply that top executives bargain less aggressively for their pay packages and leave more of a firm's revenues available for dividends or for wage increases for other employees, other people will pay taxes on that income, which offsets much of any initial loss of tax revenue. And to say the "avoidance elasticity" is high is to say there are many loopholes in the tax law—which is an argument for tightening tax

---

1. A few of the top 1% are A-list athletes or entertainers for whom competitive performance is a major motivator. It is doubtful if, when the pitch crosses the plate, any baseball player tries less hard to hit the ball because tax rates have increased.

administration. From a social perspective, the "effort elasticity" is "the sole real factor limiting optimal top tax rates" (Piketty, Saez & Santcheva, 2011: 2), and their estimate of 0.2 drives their calculation of 83 percent as the revenue-maximizing top marginal rate for the US.

The labour-supply effects of top marginal tax rates are the only true social costs of behavioural response to higher top marginal tax rates, because in this case a reduction in labour supply due to higher marginal tax rates means that output disappears. By contrast, when, in response to higher tax rates, top earners increase their avoidance or evasion of income tax, current income tax revenues decline but the income involved does not evaporate. Income that avoids taxation by a high earner this year because its reporting is delayed or because it is split with a relative taxed at a lower rate still attracts income tax. Even if income tax is entirely avoided or evaded forever, consumption and sales taxes will typically be paid when income is spent. And aside from the benefits to governments of these eventual tax revenues, net after-tax unreported income is a benefit to the individuals who receive it. Similarly, reallocation of income between managers, owners and lower-level workers affects the distribution of total income, and who pays income tax, but not the level of total income.

However, focusing on the labour-supply effects of income taxes means ignoring income from capital. In 2012, capital income comprised about a third of the declared taxable income of Canada's top 0.1 percent, a percentage that increases strongly at the very top and that has been rising over time. Hence, the closer one gets to the peak of Canada's income pyramid the less plausible is a labour-supply focus. Elsewhere (Osberg, 2008) I have noted that, in Canada, labour's share of aggregate output has been declining since 1982, while Lemieux and Riddell (forthcoming) show how that trend is accentuated if the labour income of the top 1 percent is excluded. As well, in the long term, savings from the current labour earnings of the top 1 percent will produce capital income from assets and inheritances, which will increase over time. As Piketty (2014) has emphasized, when the interest rate exceeds the growth rate (as it historically has), there is a long-run tendency for capital's share to increase. Piketty also notes that the tendency for an increasing long-run concentration of capital ownership is particularly strong when the real rate of return is higher for large wealth holders— which means inheritance becomes an increasingly important aspect of ever-growing inequality.

## Why Sharing Good Luck Can Improve Expected Well-Being

In the real world, luck matters, often a lot—a chance meeting or being in the right place at the right time can be crucially important to lifetime earnings. However, the literature discussed so far ignores uncertainty. But when high incomes are partly due to luck, what are the costs or potential benefits of sharing good luck through the tax system? An important strand in neo-classical economics emphasizes the benefits of insurance for well-being. Most people will, for example, feel better off if they buy fire insurance for their house, even if they never have a fire. Insurance is costly but greater certainty improves well-being.

Progressive taxation of income can be seen as a form of risk pooling. In the lottery of life, progressive taxation of incomes means that individuals share their good luck with others by paying more income tax in their good years and they share the good luck of others in their own bad years, by using public services paid for by other people's income taxes. A rational individual who is voting on the top marginal tax rate will compare the expected value of the public services they get during the years of low income with the expected value of the after tax income they get during their years of high income. The optimal (well-being maximizing) tax rate is a trade-off between the certain value of public services every year and the value of the chance of high after-tax individual income in lucky years.

There is no efficiency cost to taxing purely random events. Nobody turns down the big prize in a lottery, even if it is taxed. But since very high incomes also have low probability, it is reasonable for rational agents to weigh heavily the more likely outcome of a higher "social wage" of public services paid for by higher top marginal tax rates. Kindermann and Krueger (2014) develop a complex life-cycle, overlapping-generations model and calibrate it to reflect US reality. Even specifying relatively low risk aversion and assuming high labour supply effects as their preferred base case, they calculate the well-being maximizing top marginal income tax rate at 90 percent. One can summarize their results by saying that when income is uncertain, in deciding on the optimal top marginal income tax rate, a little risk aversion quantitatively offsets a lot of presumed labour supply responsiveness.

## Competitive Consumption and the Motivations of Top Earners

Although neo-classical economics assumes that individuals care only about their own consumption and never worry about comparisons with the income and consumption of others, sociologists, advertising executives and normal people have long known that this is nonsense, particularly for the very affluent. At the income levels typical of Canada's top 1 percent, and especially of the top 0.1 percent, basic needs and normal creature comforts have long ago been satisfied, so higher after-tax incomes primarily finance discretionary spending on status goods, whose major function is social ranking. And as those who attend boat shows know, the main difference between owning a 35-metre yacht and a 33-metre yacht is that the former is two metres longer, thereby demonstrating to the world that its owner is more successful and more important than the owners of smaller toys.

For taxation, the important fact about competitive consumption is that it is about relative rank; having more and bigger luxury goods compared with others, however much everyone else actually has. If everyone at the same market income level pays the same tax rate, the pecking order of relative consumption is unaffected by a decrease or increase in tax rates; tax rate changes that apply to everyone leave status rankings unchanged. However, "getting ahead" remains just as powerful a motivator at the top of the income distribution as it ever was. Before and after a tax rate change, every person still has the same incentive to want to try to "succeed." The international evidence indicates that although there are large differences across countries in the tax rates that people at the top end of the income distribution pay, top executives work hard everywhere. There are relatively small international differences in the weekly hours of work that top income earners supply (Osberg, 2003).

The implication is that there are very small costs in decreased work effort and forgone output when top marginal income tax rates are raised as long as this is done uniformly. And when status rankings that are now established using 45-, 40- and 35-metre yachts are displaced to the purchase of 35-, 30- and 25-metre boats, there may even be an environmental benefit (Osberg, 2008b).

Social Norms and Corporate Governance

In recent years, substantial scholarship has documented how CEO compensation depends on the size and scale of corporate enterprises and the mutual back-scratching of the members of compensation committees who ratify the new norms of "necessary compensation" for top executives (Gabaix & Laudier, 2008; Stiglitz, 2012). Evidence for the importance of social norms of comparison in high-end pay determination can be found in Milligan and Smart (2014), who estimated a regression model of the relationship between Canadian top 1 percent income share and top tax rates, with and without a control for the top 1 percent share in the US. Including US top pay trends in a regression with Canadian data is a test of whether top end pay rates in Canada are driven by comparisons with peers in the US. The US variables are highly significant and hugely reduce the measured impact of Canadian domestic tax rates, rendering local tax rates statistically insignificant at the standard 5 percent level. Hence, their results indicate that it is pay norms within the North American business community, and not marginal income tax rates in Canada, that primarily determine pre-tax top end incomes in Canada.

The Canadian Context: Raise My Taxes and I'll Threaten to Leave!

A perennial refrain in the Canadian financial press is that any increases in top tax rates will prompt a rush by "job creators" or "the best and the brightest" to emigrate. However, little evidence supports this assertion. Helliwell (1999, 2000) debunked the myth that lower US taxes in the 1990s created a brain drain from Canada to the US. The wider research literature on tax-induced migration was summarized by Young and Varner (2011: 258): "The consensus emerging from the migration literature—and from a range of research designs—is that people do not generally migrate in response to tax increases." Why might this be true?

Talk is cheap, but actually moving means giving up the public services that taxes pay for. Although people dislike taxes, they are the flip side of government expenditures. When comparing the pleasures of life in different places, what matters is the net advantage, counting both the cost of taxes paid and the benefits of public expenditures received. The affluent like the things that tax dollars enable, such as pothole-free roads, pleasant parks and crime-free public spaces. Most importantly, the rich can afford to live where they want to.

In 2012, Canada's top 1 percent had an average total income of $445,200 ($499,500 if capital gains are included). An income of this magnitude would enable consumption of much the same list of high-end home entertainment systems, household furnishings, luxury automobiles and other private goods anywhere in the world. Rich people everywhere are able to consume much the same items within their homes. The real differences in their quality of life emerge when they consider what they can do when they go out in public. Some of the desirable public amenities which the affluent like to enjoy, such as not being mugged or kidnapped, are the joint product of many agencies and are reasonably seen as "public goods" in the economic sense that they are generally available to all citizens.

Tax revenues also help subsidize some specifically elite activities like symphony orchestras, live theatre and the opera. Even if these activities are really publicly supported private goods that are often primarily of interest to the affluent, public subsidies are essential to their survival. Their costs are typically beyond the capability of a single patron to finance, and arguably going to the opera is a social occasion for the display of wealth. The availability of such cultural activities is an important aspect of the attractiveness for the economic elite of particular places to live, and such public spending can be seen as a return for the economic elite on their payment of higher taxes.

The sky-high real estate prices of rich neighbourhoods in Paris, London and Manhattan are concrete evidence that the affluent are willing to pay for high-quality public spaces and proximity to elite cultural services, and are not deterred by income taxes. Although one can get much more acreage for the dollar in Mogadishu than in Manhattan, rich people are not lining up to move to Somalia, despite the gulf in top marginal tax rates (0 percent vs. 51.7 percent in New York City). This is not due to differences in personal security within the home (armed guards can easily be hired in Somalia). But personal security outside the home is not as easily purchased on the private market and high quality public spaces and elite cultural services are not available in poor countries. High-end real estate prices capitalize the differences in public spaces and the net advantages for the affluent (given top income tax rates) of differing locations.

Young and Varner (2011) emphasize a different set of reasons for immobility—dislike of commuting, the cost of job changes that may accompany changes of residence and the cost of separation from family, friends and neighbourhood. However, in some contexts, such as across Swiss cantons or US metropolitan areas that bridge state lines, a remarkably short move can enable individuals to escape an increase in their taxes and plausibly keep their jobs and their friends. If little such migration within urban areas is observed when top tax rates rise in part of a city, one can expect that more costly migration in response to tax rate increases is even less likely.

In 2004, New Jersey implemented an increase of 2.6 percent in the top (over $500,000) marginal state income tax rate. None of the three other states in the Greater New York area changed tax rates at that time. As Young and Varner (2011: 260) point out, "high earners living in Bergen County, New Jersey, can move about 30 miles to Fairfield County, Connecticut, and watch their marginal (state) tax rate fall from 8.97 percent to 5 percent. Few other places in the country make it easier to move to a different state without leaving one's city or completely separating from the social ties of friends and family." Since there was no change in other New Jersey tax rates, Young and Varner were able to use this tax increase as a natural experiment and ask, using eight years of state income tax data on 40,000 taxpayers, whether there was any change in the millionaire emigration rate out of New Jersey. Specifically, they compared the emigration rate of those who experienced a tax rate increase with those who were unaffected because their incomes remained just below the $500,000 threshold. They do not estimate tax flight to be zero, and they do find that emigration is more probable among the extremely wealthy and those approaching retirement age. However, their main result is that tax flight is negligible (Young and Varner, 2011: 272). Consequently, they conclude that the 2004 increase in top tax rates raised significant ($1.08 billion) net new revenue for the state of New Jersey.

The case of New Jersey illustrates the fact that US states are quietly differentiating in top-end taxation, as Table 3.3 illustrates. Although there might be efficiency advantages to making changes to top tax rates at the national level, if national-level politics are paralyzed, change may have to come first at the local level. The Young and Varner (2011) finding of negligible impacts on migration of state level variation in top tax rates is important for the policy room of local legislators. In Canada, distances between cities are much larger, so the affluent face higher costs if they change tax jurisdictions, which implies more possibilities for within-country differentiation. In 2013, the within-country range in top marginal income tax rates was a bit larger in Canada (50.0% – 39.0% = 11.0%) than in the US (51.9% – 42.8 % = 9.1%)—a range that was largely maintained in 2016, even as top tax rates increased.

### Implications: Room to Manoeuvre on Top Tax Rates

At the federal level, there has been little progressivity in Canada's income tax system. Prior to the Liberal government's introduction in 2016 of a new top tax bracket (33 percent on income over $200,000), there were only four brackets. The top federal rate (29 percent) started well below the top 1 percent threshold (in 2015, at $138,586 taxable income), implying that there was no progressivity in tax rates at all within the top 1 percent. Income tax brackets were wide (0 to $44,701, $44,702 to $89,401, $89,402 to $138,585, and $138,586+) and the jumps in tax rate from the second (22 percent) to the third bracket marginal tax rate (26 percent) and the fourth bracket (29 percent) were modest.

How much income tax could the top 1 percent pay? Averaging over five years, 2008–2012, the top 1 percent of Canada's tax filers numbered just over 255,000 and paid an average $147,000 in federal and provincial income tax (CANSIM, 2015b). This was 33.2

percent of their reported total income, excluding capital gains, and produced $37.5 billion in tax revenue for Canada's governments. Atkinson's recommendation of a true 65 percent top marginal tax rate would therefore roughly double their current effective marginal tax rate. As noted above, moving to an effective top tax rate of 65 percent would involve (1) increasing the nominal top tax rate and (2) limiting opportunities for tax avoidance and evasion so the effective top tax rate could equal the nominal top tax rate. If Canada followed his advice, using a new tax bracket for income over $205,000, how much revenue would that produce?

Given current Canadian enforcement procedures, available data record only income now reported for income tax purposes. Working with those data arguably underestimates the tax revenue implications of higher tax rates combined with stiffer enforcement. Nevertheless, if Canada increased the top marginal tax rate to 65 percent, using a new tax bracket for income over $205,000, the mechanical calculation is to assume that no behavioural changes are induced by the tax rate increase, that is, total reported pre-tax income is unchanged. When incomes above $205,000 are taxed at 65 percent rather than at 33 percent, tax filers pay the same taxes as now on their first $205,000 and then a 65 percent tax rate on the excess over that threshold. The median member of the top 1 percent (with a total income of $289,000 before capital gains) would therefore face a tax increase of $27,700. Averaging over all 255,000 members of the top 1 percent, and assuming mechanically that all pre-tax incomes are unchanged, the increase in tax revenue on income excluding capital gains would be about $19.3 billion. When capital gains income is included, the tax revenue increases are significantly larger; the mechanical calculation produces a revenue gain of $ 26.1 billion.[2]

The more difficult issue is the plausible impact·on the tax base. Reducing the after-tax net return from pre-tax income (that is, the change from top earners keeping 67 percent of the marginal dollar of pre-tax income to keeping 35 percent) can be expected to affect the amount of income that is available to tax. The crucial

2. For details regarding this calculation, see Table 5 in Osberg (2015).

question is "How much?" As discussed above, Piketty, Saez and Stantcheva (2011, 2014) argue that the relevant elasticity is "0.2 (at most)", which means that a 50 percent change in after-tax marginal return to work time would produce a 10 percent decrease in the taxable base. If the total top 1 percent income base excluding capital gains were to shrink from its current $112.6 billion to $101.8 billion, a 65 percent rate of taxation on individual income in excess of $205,000 in this one-tenth lower tax base would then produce a net increase of $15.8 billion. The elasticity-adjusted calculation when capital gains income is included is a $21.8 billion increase. In either case, the amount of extra tax raised would grow over time as top 1 percent incomes grow.

Much of this essay has been emphasizing the "at most" part of the Piketty, Saez and Stantcheva (2011, 2014) estimate. As noted earlier, their model ignores the total time constraint on work hours. Uncertainty about incomes implies that risk-averse people will be better off even with higher tax rates. The incentive effect of competitive status consumption is unaffected when higher tax rates are uniformly applied. The more seriously one takes those arguments, the closer one's estimate of the net revenue implications of a 65 percent marginal top tax rate for Canada will be to the mechanical calculation of a net revenue impact of +$19.3 billion excluding capital gains or $26.1 billion including capital gains.

As well, since existing data on reported income has been used, neither the mechanical calculations nor the elasticity-adjusted calculations presented here can make allowance for any increased reporting of income that would come from stiffer enforcement and the limitation of tax avoidance. Increased income reporting would imply that revenue gains from higher top tax rates would be greater than the estimates reported here, but there is no way to know by what magnitude.

Total income taxes raised annually by federal, provincial and territorial governments in Canada during the 2008–12 period averaged $176.7 billion. As a percentage of total income tax revenue, increased revenue of $15.8 billion would be 8.9 percent while $26.1 billion would represent 14.8 percent, which would be serious, but not fundamental, percentage changes.

However, as more concrete comparisons, one can note that the total revenue of Canada's universities and colleges from tuition and other fees was $8.1 billion in 2012-13. Forecasted expenditures in 2014–15 on the Guaranteed Income Supplement for Canada's senior citizens were $10.1 billion. Federal support for provincial, territorial and municipal infrastructure in 2012–13 was $5 billion and international development assistance was $5.2 billion (CAN-SIM, 2015a; Global Affairs Canada, 2015; Infrastructure Canada, 2014; Service Canada, 2015). A true top marginal income tax rate of 65 percent could therefore make it possible for Canada to (1) abolish tuition for post-secondary education in Canada and (2) double federal anti-poverty spending for senior citizens or (3) double federal aid for infrastructure renewal plus double Canada's foreign aid.

Tuition-free post-secondary education and a doubling of foreign aid are, in today's political climate in Canada, examples of totally "unrealistic" scenarios. Although other OECD nations do now have adequate subway systems, tuition-free universities and respectable foreign aid budgets, these options are not seen as feasible policy alternatives in today's Canadian politics. The perceived possibilities for Canadian society are implicitly now limited by the level of taxation of Canada's top 1 percent seen as feasible. However, new possibilities open up when the menu of possible tax choices is expanded.

Conclusion
The debates on top marginal tax rates often feature overheated rhetoric, but incremental changes also soon become part of the landscape. I have calculated the revenue implications of a 65 percent marginal tax rate on income in excess of $205,000 as a sketch of possibilities but the likelihood of an abrupt shift to such tax rates in Canada's near future is zero. If increases in top marginal tax rates happen in Canada, it is far more probable that the tax room created by the combination of continuing growth of top 1 percent incomes and historically low top tax rates will be gradually encroached by incremental changes, as in the 2015/2016 federal top tax rate increase of 4 percent.

Nevertheless, doomsday predictions and howls of outrage still greet any and all proposals to increase top marginal income tax rates or to get serious about tax avoidance and evasion. Ownership of media outlets and contributions to public policy think tanks guarantee that the complaints of the affluent will be widely broadcast. However, as jurisdictions like New Jersey discover that millionaires do not, in fact, emigrate, and as high-paying industries like those in Silicon Valley and Wall Street continue to prosper in high-tax jurisdictions, some provincial and state governments may muster the nerve to implement reforms, which will make marginal changes in neighbouring jurisdictions easier.

Fundamentally, the importance of top-income taxation in Canada is not likely to go away. Over the last 30 years, middle-class incomes have stagnated while top-1-percent incomes have grown strongly. There is no clear reason why one would expect either top income growth to slow significantly and/or middle class income growth to accelerate dramatically anytime soon. Continuation of unbalanced rates of income growth imply an ever-widening gap in real incomes and an ever-greater concentration of "ability to pay" at the top of the income distribution (Osberg, 2014).

Since unbalanced growth, and increasing inequality, in market incomes has become the new normal, the political-economy question is whether continuing concentration of economic power will prevent change in top-end taxation and lock Canada ever further into accelerating inequality. Inequalities of power only partly show up in observed influence over the decisions that come up for public discussion. The more fundamental power is the ability of economic elites to define the possible policy options open for discussion and keep some issues, like higher tax rates at the top, off the policy agenda. Time will tell if this is about to change.

## References

Atkinson, A.B. (2014) "After Piketty," British Journal of Sociology 65(4), 619–638

Badel, A. & M. Huggett (2014) Taxing Top Earners: A Human Capital Perspective Working Paper 2. Revised October 2014. Federal Reserve Bank of St. Louis.

Boat Harbour Investments. 2016a. "Ontario Personal Tax Rates." http://www.tax-tips.ca/taxrates/on.htm.

Boat Harbour Investments. 2016b. "Quebec Personal Tax Rates." http://www.tax-tips.ca/taxrates/qc.htm.

Broten, Laurel C. (2014) "Charting a Path for Growth: Nova Scotia Tax and Regulatory Review," November 2014, Province of Nova Scotia, 2014

Canada Revenue Agency. 2015. "Frequently Asked Questions." http://www.cra-arc.gc.ca/gncy/nvstgtns/lds/faq-eng.html#q6.

Canada Revenue Agency. 2016. "Canadian income tax rates for individuals: Current and previous years." http://www.cra-arc.gc.ca/tx/ndvdls/fq/txrts-eng.html.

CANSIM. 2015a. "Financial information of universities and degree-granting colleges, revenues by type of funds, annually (Dollars)." Table 477-0058.

CANSIM. 2015b. "High income trends of tax filers in Canada, provinces, territories and census metropolitan areas (CMA), national thresholds, annual." Table 204-0001.

Diamond, P. & E. Saez (2011) The Case for a Progressive Tax: From Basic Research to Policy Recommendations, *Journal of Economic Perspectives*, 25, 165–90

Förster, M., A. Llena-Nozal & V. Nafilyan (2014) "Trends in Top Incomes and their Taxation in OECD Countries", OECD Social, Employment and Migration Working Papers, No. 159, OECD Publishing. http://dx.doi.org/10.1787/5jz-43jhlz87f-en

Francis, Diane (2000) Ottawa tries to cover up who's behind the $800M tax waiver: Revenue Canada manoeuvre may nix a trial. *Financial Post*, August 5, 2000.

Francis, Diane (2013) Why Are We Letting Tax Cheats Rob Canada? *National Post*. Posted: 04/05/2013.

Gabaix X. & Landier, A. (2006) "Why has CEO Pay Increased so Much?" NBER Working Paper No. 12365, July 2006, and *Quarterly Journal of Economics* (2008).

Global Affairs Canada. 2015. "International Development Project Browser." http://www.international.gc.ca/development-developpement/aidtransparency-transparenceaide/browser-banque.aspx?lang=eng.

Guvenen, Fatih, Fatih Karahan, Serdar Ozkan & Jae Song. (2015). What Do Data on Millions of US Workers Reveal about Life-Cycle Earnings Risk? Federal Reserve Bank of New York Staff Reports, no. 710, February 2015.

Heckman J.J. (1993) "What has been learned about labor supply in the last twenty years?" *American Economic Review: Papers and Proceedings* 83 (2): 116–121.

Helliwell, John F. (1999) "Checking the Brain Drain: Evidence and Implications" *Policy Options*, 6–17.

Helliwell, John F. & David Helliwell. (2000). "Tracking UBC Graduates: Trends and Explanations" *Isuma* Spring 2000: 101–110.

Infrastructure Canada (2014). "2014–2015 Report on Plans and Priorities, Section 1." http://www.infrastructure.gc.ca/pub/rpp/2014–15/2014-01-eng.html.

Internal Revenue Service (2016). "Whistleblower-Informant Award." https://www.irs.gov/uac/Whistleblower-Informant-Award.

International Monetary Fund (2013). Fiscal Monitor, October 2013. http://www.imf.org/external/pubs/ft/fm/2013/02/pdf/fm1302.pdf.

Kindermann, F. & D. Krueger (2014). High Marginal Tax Rates on the Top 1%? Lessons from a Life Cycle Model with Idiosyncratic Income Risk. NBER Working Paper No. 20601, October 2014.

Kleven, Henrik Jacobsen, Camille Landais & Emmanuel Saez (2013). "Taxation and International Migration of Superstars: Evidence from the European Football Market." *American Economic Review* 103 (5): 1892–1924

Kleven, Henrik Jacobsen, Camille Landais, Emmanuel Saez & Esben Schultz (2014). "Migration and Wage Effects of Taxing Top Earners: Evidence from the Foreigners' Tax Scheme in Denmark." *Quarterly Journal of Economics* 129(1): 333–7.

Kocieniewski, David (2012). "Whistle-Blower Awarded $104 Million by I.R.S." *New York Times* September 11, 2012. http://www.nytimes.com/2012/09/12/business/whistle-blower-awarded-104-million-by-irs.html.

Lemieux, T. & C. Riddell (2015) "Who Are Canada's Top 1 Percent?" In *Income Inequality: The Canadian Story*, edited by David A. Green, W. Craig Riddell and France St-Hilaire. The Institute for Research on Public Policy, Montreal (forthcoming).

Mackenzie H. (2015). Glory Days: CEO Pay in Canada Soaring to Pre-Recession Highs. Canadian Centre for Policy Alternatives, January 2015. https://www.policyalternatives.ca/sites/default/files/uploads/publications/National%20Office/2015/01/Glory_Days_CEO_Pay.pdf.

Milligan K. & M. Smart (2013). Provincial Taxation of High Incomes: What are the Impacts on Equity and Tax Revenue? CLSRN-IRPP Conference "Inequality in Canada: Driving Forces, Outcomes and Policy," Ottawa, February 24–25, 2013.

Milligan, K. & M. Smart (2014). "Taxation and Top Incomes in Canada." Working Paper 20489, National Bureau of Economic Research, September 2014.

Mirrlees, J. A. (1971). "An Exploration in the Theory of Optimal Income Taxation," *Review of Economic Studies*, 38, 175–208.

Osberg, L. & S. Phipps (1993). "Labour Supply with Quantity Constraints: Results from a Large Sample of Canadian Workers" *Oxford Economic Papers*, 45, 269–291.

Osberg, L. (2003). "Understanding Growth and Inequality Trends: The Role of Labour Supply in the USA and Germany," *Canadian Public Policy*, 29 (Supplement), January 2003, S163–S184.

Osberg, L. (2008a). A Quarter Century of Economic Inequality in Canada: 1981–2006. Toronto: Canadian Centre for Policy Alternatives. http://www.policyalternatives.ca/documents/National_Office_Pubs/2008/Quarter_Century_of_Inequality.pdf.

Osberg, L. (2008b) "Have most North Americans already met their Kyoto Obligations? Trends in the $CO_2$ content of Expenditure and the Role of Income Inequality." Canadian Economics Association, Vancouver, June 6, 2008.

Osberg, L. (2014). "Can Increasing Inequality Be a Steady State?" OECD Statistics Working Papers, 2014/01, OECD Publishing. http://dx.doi.org/10.1787/5jz-2bxc80xq6-en.

Osberg, L. (2015) "How Much Income Tax Could Canada's Top 1% Pay?" Canadian Centre for Policy Alternatives, Ottawa, October 2015. https://www.policyalternatives.ca/publications/reports/how-much-income-tax-could-canadas-top-1-pay.

Piketty, T. 2014. *Capital in the Twenty-First Century*. Cambridge, MA: Harvard University Press.

Piketty T. & E. Saez (2012). "Optimal Labor Income Taxation." NBER Working Paper No. 18521, November 2012, Revised December 2012 [chapter in preparation for the *Handbook of Public Economics*, Volume 5].

Piketty T., E. Saez & I. Stantcheva (2011). "Optimal taxation of top labor incomes: a tale of three elasticities," NBER Working Paper, No. 17616; (2014) American Economic Journal: Economic Policy 6(1): 230–71.

Pomerleau, K. (2014) High-Income Taxpayers Could Face a Top Marginal Tax Rate over 50 percent this Tax Season. January 23, 2014. http://taxfoundation.org/blog/high-income-taxpayers-could-face-top-marginal-tax-rate-over-50-percent-tax-season.

Prante, Gerald T. & John Austin, Top Marginal Effective Tax Rates by State and by Source of Income, 2012 Tax Law vs. 2013 Tax Law (as enacted in ATRA) (February 3, 2013). http://ssrn.com/abstract=2176526 or http://dx.doi.org/10.2139/ssrn.2176526.

Saez, E., J. Slemrod & S. H. Giertz (2012). "The Elasticity of Taxable Income with Respect to Marginal Tax Rates: A Critical Review." *Journal of Economic Literature* 50(1): 3–50

Saez, E. (2001) Using Elasticities to Derive Optimal Income Tax Rates. *The Review of Economic Studies* 68 (1): 205–229.

Saez, E. & M. R. Veall (2003). The Evolution of High Incomes in Canada, 1920–2000. NBER Working Paper No. 9607, April 2003.

Service Canada (2015). "Canada Pension Plan/Old Age Security Quarterly Report: Monthly Amounts and Related Figures from January to March 2015." http://www.servicecanada.gc.ca/eng/services/pensions/janmar15.pdf

Stiglitz J. E. (2012). *The Price of Inequality: How Today's Divided Society Endangers Our Future*. New York: W.W. Norton.

Wolfson, M., M. Veall & N. Brooks (2014). Piercing the Veil: Private Corporations and the Income of the Affluent. http://igopp.org/wp-content/uploads/2014/06/wolfson-brooks-veall_-_incomes_of_affluent.pdf.

Yakabuski, Konrad (2015). "Taxing the rich will not pay off for Trudeau." *Globe and Mail*, May 18.

# CHAPTER FOUR

# Getting to Denmark and the Top 1 Percent: Comments on Andersen and Osberg

John Myles

Beginning in the 1970s, sociologists became fascinated by the welfare state explosion of the post-war decades. Why had this happened? Why are some welfare states more luxurious than others? Why do welfare states spend their money in different ways? Only rarely did we ask questions about the politics of revenue-raising for these projects, that is, taxation. Sociologists are generally quick to advocate more spending in policy domains that affect the subjects of their research (and more research dollars). Rarely, however, do they include a discussion of where the additional dollars should come from.

All that has begun to change. Under the label of the "new fiscal sociology" (Martin, Mehrota & Prasad, 2009), a younger generation of US sociologists has been working hard on taxation politics. In 2014, Monica Prasad (2012) won the American Sociological Association's best-book award for her work on the topic. For aspiring scholars, the politics of Canada's taxation system is ripe for the taking. Good places to begin include Rod Haddow's superb *Comparing Ontario and Quebec: Political Economy and Public Policy at the Turn of the Millennium* (2015) and Alex Himmelfarb and Jordan Himmelfarb's (2013) *Tax is Not a Four Letter Word*.

As with many topics that involve money, sociologists have to master what the economists have to say about taxation systems before moving on to ask questions about taxation politics. Lars Osberg takes up some of the standard objections to higher marginal tax rates for top earners. Would higher taxes encourage top income earners to work fewer hours or with less intensity and commitment? Would they all move to the United States? Would their accountants just sharpen their pencils and find new tax avoidance strategies? He concludes on each count that the answer is no.

He estimates that a 65 percent marginal rate on incomes above $205,000 would add between $15.8 and $26.1 billion to the government coffers without inflicting any meaningful social damage. The probability of moving to a 65 percent rate any time soon is close to zero according to Osberg and I agree. But the point is that given existing top rates of about 50 percent governments have lots of room to manoeuvre and that's important. It means that Prime Minister Trudeau's 4 percent tax increase for the top 1 percent could be repeated again in the future.

Osberg's paper raises important questions for political sociology. The most obvious question is whether raising top marginal rates is politically feasible. I think it is. While writing a paper with Keith Banting last year we learned that several provinces had already introduced small tax increases on top earners.[1] What amazed us was that we'd never heard of these changes either in the media or from the usual political lobbies for the needy rich. The political backlash was minimal. My best guess is that the marginal gains top earners might have won from making a fuss was not worth the potential embarrassment given the bad publicity they've received in recent years. The backlash from the introduction of Prime Minister Trudeau's new tax bracket has also been surprisingly muted.

Now to my main point: Will raising taxes on the top 1 percent move us closer to Denmark? I am sceptical. My main concern is that raising rates on top earners isn't going to move the dial on income inequality very much. Nor will it provide the revenues

1. The Ontario government introduced modest tax increases on high-income earners in 2012 and 2014. The 2012 increase affected the top 0.2 percent of tax filers, while the 2014 increase affected the top 2 percent of income earners—those with taxable income over $150,000. In 2015, in the face of steep declines in resource revenues, budgets in both Alberta and Newfoundland and Labrador also introduced new tax brackets for higher income earners, in Alberta's case phasing out its symbolic flat tax.

## Figure 4.1. The Puzzle of Tax and Welfare Systems

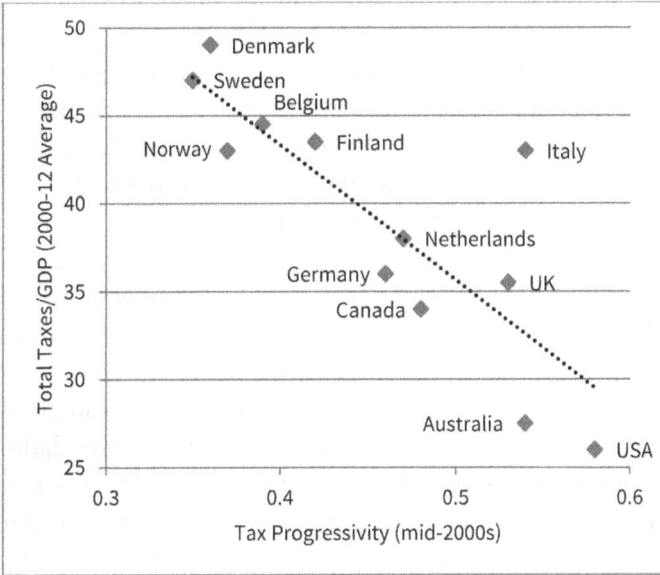

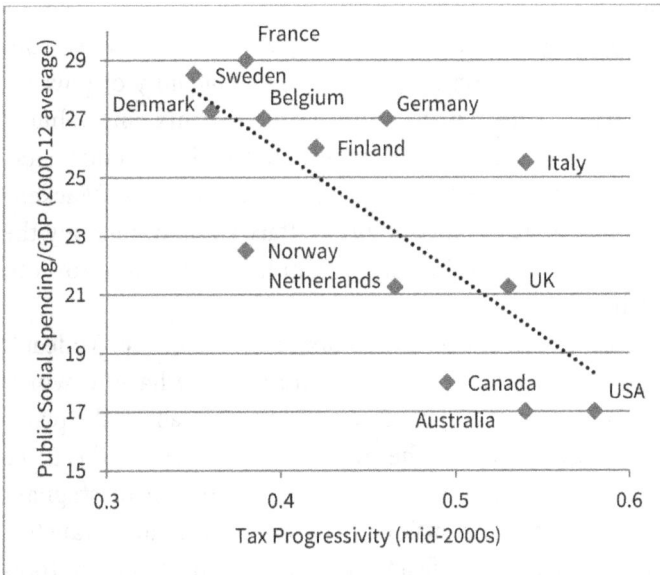

*Source: Charts based on Alexander Hertel-Fernandez and Cathie Jo Martin, "How employers and conservatives shaped the modern tax state," unpublished paper, Boston University, 2015. Authors' analysis of OECD data.*

required to do all the good things that need doing with respect to things like global warming, affordable housing, childcare and public transit.

Sixteen to 26 billion dollars is not to be sneezed at but, as Osberg points out, it does not represent a fundamental change to a federal tax budget of some $280 billion. Nor will it compensate for the tax cuts of the past several decades. Total government revenue from all levels of government has declined from about 44 percent to 38 percent of GDP since the late 90s. That's going to be tough to get back.

If we want to get to Denmark, as Robert Andersen would have us do, we have to tax like Denmark or at least move in that direction. As Figure 4.1 shows, we have a long way to go. And as the data also indicate, to get there we'll probably have to give up some of our attachment to the sacred cow of tax progressivity. Indeed, the big puzzle of taxation systems is that countries with high levels of taxation and social spending rely mainly on regressive payroll and consumption taxes on labour while taxes on capital are modest. The low spending US wins the beauty contest for the most progressive tax system.

Lane Kenworthy (2012: 75) shows that what matters most from the point of view of income inequality is the *quantity* of government revenues, not the progressivity of the tax mix since almost all redistribution occurs on the spending, not the revenue, side. Regressive taxes can be used for progressive purposes (Mackenzie, 2013). High tax revenues and big welfare states are mainly the product of within-class solidarity, not more successful efforts to soak the rich.

To get to Denmark, we'll have to tax Prime Minister Trudeau's "middle class" a lot more, not less. To do that, we have to worry more about middle-class earnings. For all the talk about the problems of the middle class in the 2015 federal election, the three national parties carefully avoided the core problem of stagnant middle-class earnings. Attention focused on taxes and transfers since Ottawa still has significant control over these policy tools while labour market policy is under provincial jurisdiction.

As Lucy Goodhart (2015) shows, however, public tolerance for higher taxes depends critically on labour market performance. The *sine qua non* for popular support for higher taxes for almost everyone is a sustained period of serious wage growth for almost everyone. Given stagnant or declining wages, the only mechanisms that lower and middle-income workers can use to boost consumption are to vote for a lower tax rate and/or to take on debt. Goodhart concludes that, since the median voter is a lower or middle-income worker, the preference for lower taxes tends to get enacted and household debt levels are at an all-time high.

The Liberal Party offered the winning platform of a middle-class tax cut in the 2015 election. The cut was only partially offset by a rate increase on the top 1 percent, thereby eroding the new government's revenue base and moving us further from Denmark. The estimated annual loss to the treasury ($1.2 billion in 2016–17) is modest relative to total revenue. Nevertheless, offsetting wage stagnation with tax cuts is not a strategy that can be repeated endlessly over future election cycles without eroding the revenue base required to finance ambitious policy goals regarding the environment, public transit, child care and economic inequality.

Osberg shows that Canada still has plenty of room to tax the rich and I agree. But selling the "middle class" on the benefits of better public services, more equality or a greener economy with the argument that someone else will pay for it is selling an illusion. To get to Denmark, as Mathew Yglesias (2015) argues, Canadians may even have to take on the Danish idea that "the middle class should agree to pay high taxes because public services are more valuable than additional private consumption." During rush hour, rapid public transit trumps the new Ferrari.

## References

Goodhart, Lucy. 2015. "Where Is the Political Response to Inequality in the Us?" Paper presented at the Annual Meetings of the American Political Science Association, San Francisco.

Haddow, Rodney. 2015. *Comparing Quebec and Ontario: Political Economy and Public Policy at the Turn of the Millennium.* Toronto: University of Toronto Press.

Himmelfarb, Alex & Jordan Himmelfarb, eds. 2013. *Tax Is Not a Four-Letter Word: A Different Take on Taxes in Canada.* Waterloo, ON: Wilfrid Laurier University Press.

Mackenzie, Hugh. 2013. "Taxes and Public Services." In A. Himmelfarb & J. Himmelfarb, eds., *Tax Is Not a Four-Letter Word.* Waterloo, ON: Wilfrid Laurier University Press.

Martin, Isaac, Ajay Mehrota & Monica Prasad, eds. 2009. *The New Fiscal Sociology:*

*Taxation in Comparative and Historical Perspective.* New York: Cambridge University Press.

Prasad, Monica. 2012. *The Land of Too Much: American Abundance and the Paradox of Poverty.* Cambridge MA: Harvard University Press.

Yglesias, Mathew. 2015. "9 Questions about Denmark: Bernie Sanders's Favorite Socialist Utopia." Vox. http://www.vox.com/2015/10/16/9544007/denmark-nordic-model.

CHAPTER FIVE

# How Welfare State Policy Contributes to Gender Equality and Inequality: A Comparative Perspective

Ito Peng

## Introduction

It is difficult to make a universally valid generalization about the contribution of welfare state policy to gender equality and inequality. What can be said with confidence is that welfare states can contribute to both gender inequality and gender equality, depending on how policy makers design them (Lewis, 1998; O'Connor, Orloff & Shaver, 1999; Sainsbury, 1999). The picture is complex because many policies affect gender equality and inequality; policies often contravene one another; and numerous factors beyond welfare state policy are involved in the process of achieving gender equality.

In the mainly rich countries that belong to the Organization for Cooperation and Development (OECD), a gradual shift toward greater gender equality may be observed over the last several decades, though the speed of that change is slow in most cases and the specifics of the change vary from country to country. The most gender-equal countries are in Scandinavia. They also have large welfare states. The World Economic Forum's 2014 Global Gender Gap Index measures, for each country, the gap between women and men in economic participation and opportunity, educational attainment, health and survival, and political empowerment. The five countries with the smallest gender gap are Iceland, Finland, Norway, Sweden and Denmark, in that order (Table 5.1). These countries often are referred to as social-democratic welfare states.

Rich English-speaking countries such as New Zealand, Canada, the United States, Australia and the United Kingdom—countries that are often grouped as liberal welfare states—rank between thirteenth and twenty-sixth. Because social democratic welfare states enjoy larger and more generous welfare state provisions than do liberal welfare states, logic would suggest that generous welfare states are associated with greater gender equality. While that is generally the case, we find the picture is more complex if we examine Table 5.1 more closely. Thus, between the five social-democratic welfare states and the five liberal welfare states, one funds a cluster of relatively big welfare states, such as Belgium (10), Switzerland (11), Germany (12), the Netherlands (14), and France (16), as well as small welfare states such as Nicaragua (6), Rwanda (7) and the Philippines (9).

At the same time, some welfare states that are more generous than those of Canada or the US are ranked lower on the gender gap index. This group includes Luxembourg (28), Spain (29) and Italy (69). Finally, some countries lie far below the others in terms of gender gap index. Japan (104) and South Korea (117) are notable members of this group. A comparison of these two countries also shows that Japan has a much higher level of welfare state spending (23.9 percent of GDP) than does South Korea (10.4 percent), yet both are low on the gender equality index. In short, the correlation between gender gap rank and welfare state generosity is far from perfect.

So then how is welfare state policy related to gender equality? The answer is: While some welfare state policies contribute to gender equality, other welfare state policies create barriers to gender equality. Accordingly, in the balance of this paper, I focus on two questions: (1) Exactly how do welfare state policies contribute to gender equality and inequality? (2) How do social contexts influence welfare state policies and gender equality? As we shall see, the second question highlights the fact that changing social and economic contexts require us to think not only about inequality between groups (men and women) but also within groups (women).

### The Welfare State and Its Relationship to Gender

Gøsta Esping-Andersen (1985) famously argued that the welfare state is a battle of "politics against markets." In order for the state to protect and promote the social and economic well-being of its citizens, it must help individuals de-commodify some of their labour so that they are not entirely dependent on the labour market for their economic survival. To achieve that goal, the welfare state must rely on a system of social and economic redistribution. It must aim to reduce social and economic disparities between rich and poor. In capitalist democracies, welfare states do this by means of taxation and public transfers, the latter including employment insurance, health and medical insurance, pensions, social welfare payments, education, public housing, childcare support, family allowances, and so on.

In the process of structuring redistributive systems, the welfare state also shapes class and social structures. In the 1980s and 1990s, mainstream welfare state theorists noted that different welfare regimes

Table 5.1.

Gender Gap Index and Public Social Expenditures as Percent of GDP, Selected Countries (most recent year available)

| Country | Gender Gap (rank) | Public Social Expenditures (% GDP) |
|---|---|---|
| Iceland | 1 | 16.5 |
| Finland | 2 | 31.0 |
| Norway | 3 | 22.0 |
| Sweden | 4 | 28.1 |
| Denmark | 5 | 30.1 |
| Nicaragua | 6 | 13.0 |
| Rwanda | 7 | 7.5 |
| Ireland | 8 | 21.0 |
| Philippines | 9 | 4.9 |
| Belgium | 10 | 30.7 |
| Switzerland | 11 | 19.4 |
| Germany | 12 | 25.8 |
| New Zealand | 13 | 20.8 |
| Netherlands | 14 | 24.7 |
| Latvia | 15 | 15.0 |
| France | 16 | 31.7 |
| Burundi | 17 | 9.3 |
| South Africa | 18 | 8.7 |
| Canada | 19 | 17.0 |
| United States | 20 | 19.2 |
| Australia | 24 | 19.0 |
| Great Britain | 26 | 21.7 |
| Luxembourg | 28 | 23.5 |
| Spain | 29 | 26.8 |
| Italy | 69 | 28.6 |
| Japan | 104 | 23.9 |
| South Korea | 117 | 10.4 |

*Sources: World Economic Forum (2015); OECD (2016e); OECD (2016e); Asian Development Bank (2015); CEPALSTAT (2015); National Institute for Population and Social Security Research (2014).*

lead to different social and economic stratification outcomes. The most popular welfare regimes theory, that of Esping-Andersen (1990), highlights three main types of welfare regimes—social democratic, conservative, and liberal.

Social-democratic welfare regimes are characterized by generous and universal welfare provisions, whereas conservative welfare regimes are recognized by generous but particularistic and status-differentiated welfare provisions. Liberal welfare regimes rely more heavily on the market to provide welfare and therefore tend to provide limited and selective welfare support, often in the form of poverty relief. Social-democratic welfare states such as Denmark, Sweden, Finland and Norway, and conservative welfare states such as Belgium, France and Germany, tend to have high public social expenditures as a percentage of GDP. Liberal welfare states such as the US, Canada, Australia and the UK tend to have low public social expenditures as a percentage of GDP.

Countries with relatively generous welfare states tend to enjoy comparatively low levels of income inequality as measured by the Gini index. For the 20 richest OECD countries, the correlation between welfare state expenditures and the Gini index is −.349 (calculated from OECD, 2016b; 2016e; United Nations Development Report, 2015).

Feminist scholars argue that, in addition to shaping class structures, welfare state policies also influence gender relations, thus contributing to gender equality and inequality (Fraser, 1994; Lewis, 1992; Orloff, 1993; Sainsbury, 1999). That is because different welfare state architectures are premised on different ideas about gender and family relations. For example, social democratic welfare states were built on the premise of an "adult-worker" household model, meaning it is assumed that both men and women will be working throughout most of their adult lives and contributing equally to domestic labour. Because of this assumption, social-democratic welfare states tend to offer more support for women and single mothers to participate in the labour market than do others types of welfare state. They do this through public childcare and elder care provisions that relieve mothers and women of unpaid family care responsibilities that create barriers to employment. In addition, because social-democratic welfare states do not assume that households are composed of male breadwinners and female housewives, they are more accepting of single-mother households and provide relatively generous income support, education and training for them.

In contrast, liberal welfare states have traditionally adhered to a "male-breadwinner/female-housewife" household model. They are therefore not as supportive towards women, particularly married women. Although in recent decades most liberal welfare states have shifted to the adult-worker household model, because of their market-based approach to social welfare they are less generous than are social democratic welfare states when it comes to advancing childcare, elder care and other work-family reconciliation policies. Consequently, in liberal welfare states, the employment rate of women is relatively high but maternal employment rates are relatively low because the enrolment rate of preschool age children in early childhood education and care programs is comparatively low. In social-democratic welfare states, the employment rate of women is relatively high but so are maternal employment rates and rates of enrolment of preschool age children in early childhood education and care programs (OECD, 2016d).

As these facts amply demonstrate, welfare-state type powerfully affects gender equality and inequality. We see that when welfare state policies are aimed at supporting women's employment and reducing their care burden they can result in more gender-equal outcomes.

### Welfare State Policies and Their Gendered Outcomes

Specifically, the following welfare state policies are associated with gender equality and inequality outcomes:

- Equal employment opportunity legislation;
- Equal pay and pay equity legislation;
- Work-family reconciliation policies such as parental leave, child care, child care leave and elder care;
- Anti-discrimination policies;
- Employment protection legislation;
- Extension of social insurance and social protection to non-standard workers;

- Income support policies such as social welfare, elderly support and family allowance;
- Pension policy;
- Education policy;
- Gender quota policy, such as having a set percentage of women on company boards, in government offices, in political parties and so on.

To illustrate the impact of just one item on this non-exhaustive list, consider how pension policy influences gender equality. In Canada and elsewhere, employee pension schemes are tied to formal, often full-time employment. They are based on people's wages. However, women's wages are typically lower than men's wages. Until recently, many women did not work outside the home after they married and/or had children. Even today, the labour force participation rate is lower for women than for men. When women work outside the home, they tend to hold low-wage, non-standard, and precarious jobs. Consequently, women in Canada and many other countries typically contribute less to pensions than men do, so they receive smaller pensions in retirement compared to men.

These gender biases are built into the pension system because they were developed at a time when it was assumed that only the husband would work in the paid labour force, that the divorce rate would remain low and that, after retirement, husband and wife would continue living together and sharing the husband's pension. In 2011, the average gender pension gap for 25 OECD countries was 28 percent, ranging from just over 5 percent for Estonia to nearly 45 percent for Germany (Figure 5.1). Most of the variation in the size of the gap can be explained by the extent to which a country follows the male-breadwinner household model. Unfortunately, good data on the gender pension gap in Canada does not exist, but it is likely that the figure for Canada is in the same ballpark as that for other countries following the male-breadwinner household model, such as the US (with a gap of nearly 35 percent) and the UK (nearly 40 percent). We thus see that, although pension policies may at first seem to have nothing to do with gender equality, the structure of pension policies contributes heavily to differential economic outcomes for men and women.

In general, type of welfare regime affects gender equality and inequality in discernible ways. First, social democratic welfare states tend to have the most extensive policies related to equal employment and equal pay legislation, family-work reconciliation and social care policies such as public child care and elder care, more generous income support and pensions, and clear gender quota policies. They also have the most gender-neutral pension schemes. These factors all lead to more gender-equal outcomes.

Second, many liberal welfare states have good equal employment and pay legislation but inferior social care policies. Because services such as childcare and elder care are often left to the family

Figure 5.1. Average Pension Gender Gap (%) on Total Pension Income, 2011

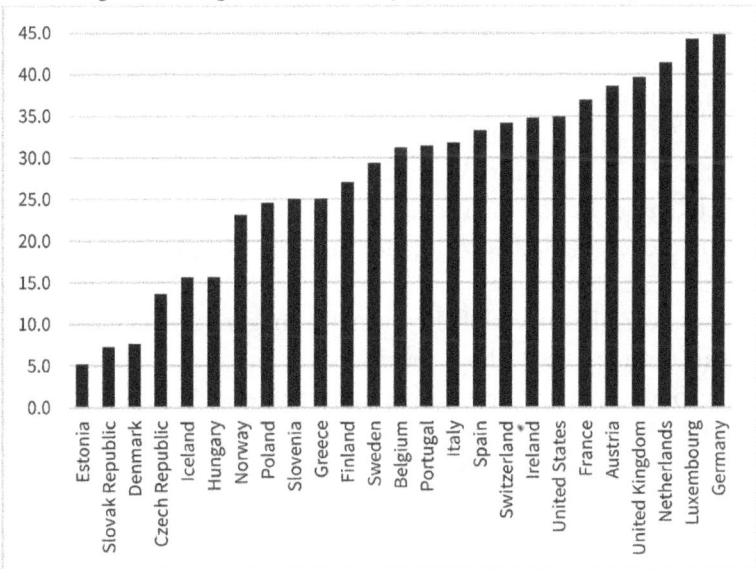

Note: *United States data are for 2010. Source: OECD (2016c).*

and the market, these countries tend to privilege higher income families that can afford private childcare and elder care. This situation creates barriers to gender equality insofar as the burden of care falls largely on women and families, in turn making it difficult for women to compete on an equal footing with men in the labour market. In addition, this context creates inequality between women with post-secondary education and high earnings, and other women.

Third, in countries like Japan and South Korea, where governments invest more in public childcare and elder care but fail to provide adequate muscle to employment and pay equity legislation, we find the perpetuation of gender inequality in terms of wages, working conditions and social security, and increasing inequality between the small proportion of highly educated and well-paid women who follow a "male" career trajectory (and are treated like men) and other women who must contend with a "female" career trajectory, meaning lower wages, less job security, and less social security.

### How New Social and Economic Contexts Contribute to Between- and Within-Group Inequalities

In the last decade or so, many OECD countries have tried to address gender equality issues, partly because women have mobilized to further their interests and partly because new global norms, such as the 2008 UN Convention on the Elimination of All Forms of Discrimination against Women, have pressured governments to act. These are the main reasons why the gender wage gap has declined over the last few decades in almost all OECD countries (Figure 5.2).

However, the new global concern over gender equality is not driven entirely, or perhaps even mainly, by altruism. Structural and economic factors are pushing governments to pursue gender equality. Today, family structures are more diverse than they were half a century ago. Employment is more precarious. Global economic competition is more intense. Economic crises are deeper. Consequently, societies can no longer depend on the male breadwinner husband for the family's economic security. Today, in every OECD country, most families need two income earners. Thus, the male-breadwinner household model no longer works well and we are moving to the adult-worker household model. Where it has become imperative for men and women to work in the paid labour force, it makes economic and political sense for the state to ensure greater gender equality. As women's educational levels increase, it also makes economic sense for the state and employers to mobilize and utilize women's human capital.

Even the most sexist welfares states, such as those of Japan and South Korea, have begun to make gender equality a key part of their social policy agenda. In Japan, for example, Prime Minister Abe—one of the most conservative prime ministers in Japan's recent history—proclaimed a "three arrows" strategy in 2012 to get the country out of its decades-long economic slump. The strategy involves massive monetary stimulus, increased government spending, and social and economic policy reforms, chief among which are policies aimed at supporting women, including more support for childcare and elder care, active employment policies for women, and 30 percent target quotas for women managers and board members in companies. He calls this approach "womanomics."

I am pretty sure Mr. Abe did not arrive at this policy reform because he suddenly became a feminist. To the contrary, he is about as likely to become a feminist as I am to join the Wild Rose Party. Mr. Abe is setting in motion a set of policies that will support women in the labour market precisely because he realizes that the Japanese economy needs women's human capital. His gender policies therefore constitute a win-win strategy for economic growth and public support.

As more countries increasingly attend to gender equality, particularly as measured in terms of women's labour market participation, I suggest that it is necessary to pay more attention to within-group inequalities, that is, inequalities between categories of women, and not just between men and women.

Growing income inequality in OECD countries since the early 1990s has been played out not only between men and women but also among women, partly because of the increased premium placed on higher education, partly because of a growing tendency toward assortative mating, in which mates are increasingly likely to have similar educational credentials. Additionally, these variables increasingly intersect with race, ethnicity and immigration status. We may celebrate the fact that women have made advances over the last few decades in chipping away at the glass ceiling. Today, we see more women in government bureaucracy, political leadership roles, and company management. In addition, many more women are attending university and becoming professionals than was the case a generation ago.

What is troubling is that while women have been able to make these advances, the basic game plan has remained the same. By this I mean that women are making advances by following exactly the same rules that conform to pre-existing gender relations. These rules favour so-called productive wage labour outside of the home and undervalue reproductive care work that is carried out in the household. Put another way, most women executives and political leaders are able to work and succeed because they have other

Figure 5.2. Gender Wage Gap, Selected Countries, 2001-13
(percentage change between 2001 and 2013 indicated)

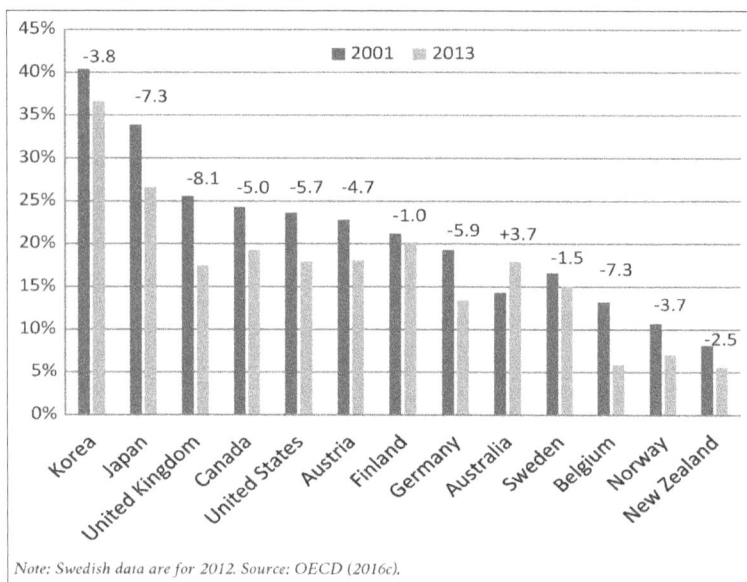

Note: Swedish data are for 2012. Source: OECD (2016c).

people—almost always other women—taking care of their children, cleaning their houses, and perhaps also cooking meals for their families. What we have here is the continuation of a gender division of labour in which some women are, like men, becoming dependent on the reproductive work of other women to succeed in their productive work. Moreover, the women who are doing such reproductive caring work are increasingly drawn from immigrant and ethnic minority communities.

In pushing more women forward, we neglected to restructure the basic game plan of gender relations. Therefore we now have not just gender inequality; we have more complicated forms of between and within-group gender inequalities that are formed along the productive-reproductive work divide.

In sum, welfare state policies can contribute to gender equality as well as inequality, depending on what those policies aim to do, and depending on what kinds of gender models these policies are premised on. Moreover, given that our social and economic contexts have changed dramatically over the last several decades, we need to re-examine the state of gender equality/inequality today and to think not only about between-group but also within-group inequalities. An especially fruitful approach to the study of welfare state policies and gender equality would be to investigate how new social and economic contexts contribute to different forms of inequalities between women along racial, ethnic and immigration lines.

## References

Asian Development Bank. 2015. "Key Indicators for Asia and Pacific 2015." http://www.adb.org/publications/key-indicators-asia-and-pacific-2015.

CEPALSTAT (Economic Commission for Latin America and the Caribbean). 2015. "Database and Statistical Publications." http://estadisticas.cepal.org/cepalstat/web_cepalstat/Portada.asp?idioma=i.

Esping-Andersen, Gøsta. 1985. *Politics against Markets: The Social Democratic Road to Power*. Princeton, NJ: Princeton University Press.

Esping-Andersen, Gøsta. 1990. *The Three Worlds of Welfare Capitalism*. Princeton, NJ: Princeton University Press.

Fraser, Nancy. 1994. "After the Family Wage: Gender Equality and Welfare State." *Political Theory* 22(4): 591–618.

Lewis, Jane. 1992. "Gender and the Development of Welfare Regimes." *Journal of European Social Policy* 2(3): 159–173.

Lewis, Jane, (Ed.). 1998. *Gender, Social Care and Welfare State Restructuring in Europe*. Aldershot, UK: Ashgate.

National Institute for Population and Social Security Research. 2015. "Japanese Social Security Statistics." http://www.ipss.go.jp/ssj-db/e/ssj-db-top-e.asp.

OECD. 2016a. "Employment: Gender Wage Gap." http://stats.oecd.org/index.aspx-?queryid=54751.

OECD. 2016b. "Inequality." https://data.oecd.org/inequality/income-inequality.htm.

OECD. 2016c. "New OECD data and analysis revealing the wide gap in pension benefits between men and women." http://www.oecd.org/gender/data/newoecddataandanalysisrevealingthewidegapinpensionbenefitsbetweenmenandwomen.htm.

OECD. 2016d. "OECD Family Database." http://www.oecd.org/els/family/database.htm.

OECD. 2016e. "Social Expenditure Database (SOCX)." http://www.oecd.org/els/soc/expenditure.htm.

O'Connor, Julia S., Ann S. Orloff & Sheila Shaver. 1999. *States, Markets, Families: Gender, Liberalism and Social Policy in Australia, Canada, Great Britain and the United States*. Cambridge UK: Cambridge University Press.

Orloff, Ann Shola. 1993. "Gender and Social Rights of Citizenship: The Comparative Analysis of Gender Relations and Welfare States." *American Sociological Review* 58(3): 303–328.

Sainsbury, Diane. 1999. *Gender and Welfare State Regimes*. Oxford: Oxford University Press.

United Nations Development Report. 2015. "Income Gini Coefficient." http://hdr.undp.org/en/content/income-gini-coefficient.

World Economic Forum. 2015. "The Global Gender Gap Report 2014." http://reports.weforum.org/global-gender-gap-report-2014/.

CHAPTER SIX

# What is the Role of Early Childhood Education and Care in an Equality Agenda?

Gordon Cleveland

## Introduction

More than three decades ago, Supreme Court Justice Rosalie Abella (1984) wrote that "child care is the ramp that provides equal access to the workforce for mothers." When child care is more affordable, women can earn income and care for children, reducing the exclusion of mothers from employment and reducing the gender gap in wages, occupational segregation, and the threat of poverty when marriages break up and when women are elderly and alone.

This chapter analyzes the contribution of early childhood education and care services (ECEC) in Canada to gender equity and to reducing child outcome disparities and family income disparities among children and families from different socio-economic backgrounds. Most people believe that early childhood education and care is good for children; we know that it promotes children's cognitive and social development, particularly when the quality of care is high. Because ECEC is especially beneficial for vulnerable children who are more likely to be from lower-income backgrounds, we believe that universal access to child care and kindergarten services should help to flatten the socio-economic gradient in children's abilities and outcomes. Finally, it is widely believed that, insofar as affordable child care increases women's employment, work experience and earnings, it should contribute to a reduction in income inequality between families and a reduction in child poverty.

However, as American folk philosopher and satirist Henry

Wheeler Shaw is reputed to have said: "It ain't so much the things we don't know that get us into trouble, it's the things we do know that just ain't so." In important respects, our shared view of the success of early childhood education and care in fostering equality in Canada is wrong or at least overly optimistic. This chapter will make the case that early childhood education and care policy still has important work to do if it is to fulfill its promise of contributing fully to an equality agenda.

ECEC refers to publicly regulated and subsidized or publicly-provided child care and early education services for children before they enter Grade 1, at five or six years of age. It includes licensed care in child care centres and licensed or regulated home-based care and care in nursery schools or preschools. It also encompasses part-day or full-day care in kindergartens that are part of the public school system. In most provinces, kindergartens are mainly for five-year-old children. In Ontario, junior kindergarten covers children four years of age and some who are nearly four. Because of data availability, however, many of the tables in this chapter refer to regulated child care services only and do not include kindergarten.

In this chapter I focus on gender equity in families, employment and society, and child and family equity. I do not address differences between the abilities of boys and girls, between children from recent immigrant backgrounds and those whose families have been in Canada for a longer time, and between children with varying levels of disability and ability. ECEC policy should take these aspects of equity into account as well.

This chapter will marshal evidence about whether ECEC in Canada is making the contribution to gender, child and family equity that it is capable of making. Lack of high quality evidence establishing causal connections between the state of ECEC services and gender, child and family inequality means that my conclusions will be suggestive, not definitive. There is much room for research in this field.

My main argument is that we have witnessed a dramatic expansion in ECEC in Canada over the past 20 years and we should therefore be able to observe much progress in the reduction of different forms of inequality. Some evidence of progress in this regard exists. However, disparities are still wide. I uncover evidence that not enough lower-income families are gaining access to ECEC services to have made a big difference in equalizing child outcomes and family incomes. I conclude by discussing the types of ECEC policies that are most likely to increase success in narrowing such inequalities.

## The Expansion of ECEC in Canada

Table 6.1 summarizes the expansion of regulated child care in Canada between 1994–95 and 2010–11. In brief, the percentage of employed and studying mothers using regulated child care more than doubled over the 16-year period, from 19 percent to 46 percent. The percentage using unregulated care (informal, unlicensed child care) fell by more than half, from 45 percent to 22 percent. The percentage of mothers relying exclusively on parental care declined only slightly by 4 percentage points, from 36 percent to 32 percent.

Increased use of regulated care occurred across all kinds of families, not just urban, married families with Canadian-born parents. Specifically, the percentage of families using regulated care more than doubled between 1994–95 and 2010–11 among immigrant families, families headed by a lone mother, rural and small town families, families outside Quebec who speak mainly French and families in Quebec who speak mainly English. Only among lone-mother families, where the percentage using licensed child care was already high in 1994–95, did the percentage using regulated care not double (Cleveland and Forer, 2010).

| Table 6.1. Patterns of Child Care Use by Employed or Studying Mothers, Canada (in percent) | | | | |
|---|---|---|---|---|
| Care Type/ Year | Regu- lated | Unregu- lated | Paren- tal | Total |
| 1994–95 | 19 | 45 | 36 | 100 |
| 2006–07 | 41 | 30 | 30 | 101* |
| 2010–11 | 46 | 22 | 32 | 100 |

*Due to rounding.*
*Source: Cleveland & Forer (2010).*

A major reason for the shift from unregulated to regulated care was the introduction in Quebec of regulated child care services at a user cost of $7 per day and free full-day kindergarten for 5-year-olds. However, the use of regulated child care increased dramatically in Canada outside of Quebec too (Cleveland et al., 2008). I conclude that if ECEC is failing to have a large impact on inequality, it is not because parents are rejecting regulated care.

## Change in Gender Inequality

If early childhood education and care services contribute to gender equity by providing a ramp into employment, and into full-time employment rather than part-time employment, and into "good" jobs rather than "bad" jobs, then we should expect large reductions in gender inequality to have occurred in recent decades. As the use of early childhood education and care has grown, has gender equity improved?

Over the past few decades, a massive influx of women into the paid labour force has occurred. In the 1970s, fewer than half of women between the ages of 25 and 54 were in the paid labour force. Today, the figure is over 75 percent (Vincent, 2013). In the 1970s, only about one-third of mothers with children under the age of 6 were in the paid labour force. Today, the figure is more than 73 percent (Friendly et al., 2013).

The educational attainment of women has also proceeded apace. Women between the ages of 25 and 54 are now more likely to have post-secondary education than are men (TD Economics, 2007). Women are moving into the entire range of professions and highly skilled occupations. Nonetheless, most women are still concentrated in a small number of occupations in the workforce; in 2009, two-thirds of female workers were employed in teaching, nursing and health care, office and administrative work, and sales and service (Vincent, 2013). Fewer than one-third of men were in these broad occupational groups, which include many modestly paid occupations.

As in employment and education, so in wages: In 1988, the average hourly wage of full-time female workers was only 76 percent that of men. By 2011, the comparable figure was 87 percent (Vincent, 2013). A substantial gender wage gap exists, but it is narrowing (Fortin & Schirle, 2007).

An important part of the gender gap in pay is the family gap, the difference in hourly pay between women with children and women without children (Waldfogel & Pal, 2014; Waldfogel, 1998;

Vincent, 2013). Women with children who are in the paid labour force earn less than do women without children who are in the paid labour force. The family gap in annual income for full-time women workers with the same level of education and the same amount of job experience is more than 17 percent (Phipps et al., 2001). It is possible that having children affects mothers' productivity in employment, but even when adjustments are made for this possibility there is an 8 percent gap in income between women who have children and work full-time and women who have no children and work full-time.

A strong time pattern exists in the family pay gap (Zhang, 2008). The size of the gap is 30 percent to 40 percent during the year a child is born and very substantial in the following year. The motherhood gap in pay only disappears at the seventh year after the child's birth. The gap is much bigger for working mothers who change employers after the birth of a child.

The OECD does a different calculation: the gender gap in pay between women and men who do not have children compared to the gender gap in pay between women and men who do have children. They report that the gender wage gap for women without children in Canada is about 6.5 percent but for women with children, the gender wage gap is an astonishing 29 percent (Vincent, 2013).

Little research has been conducted on the family pay gap in Canada but it is believed to be strongly associated with the burden of child rearing that falls particularly on women and affects many of their employment-related decisions. Women with children often take jobs that permit them to take major responsibility for child rearing—typically, part-time jobs, self-employment, contractual and short-term employment and jobs with flexible hours. In Canada on average, women with children spend more than 50 hours per week caring for their children while men spend fewer than half these hours caring for their children (Vincent, 2013).

In sum, although substantial progress toward decreasing gender inequality has been made, considerable employment and wage inequality associated with family roles still exists, especially for women with young children.

What is the state of child and family inequality in Canada? Are child outcome gradients getting flatter? Are family incomes rising for low-income families, those with low levels of education or facing some other sort of disadvantage?

There exists a child outcomes gap between children in families at different levels of socio-economic status (SES). Not all vulnerable children are in low-income families but in low-income families there is a larger percentage of children who are vulnerable and the depth and multiplicity of vulnerabilities are likely to be greater.

This pattern is not unique to Canada; it is evident in research in most advanced economies. Substantial gaps exist between children from different backgrounds across multiple domains including academic achievement, verbal ability, intelligence, vocabulary and literacy (Bradley and Corwyn, 2002; Nicholson et al., 2012). These associations are persistent in the medium to long term, with low income during childhood predicting adult outcomes including earnings, working hours use of welfare and health (Conti & Heckman, 2012; Duncan, Ziol-Guest & Kalil, 2010).

The mechanisms by which income affects children's development are less clear. Six possible pathways exist: home environment, quality of child care received outside the home, perceived economic pressure/stress, parental mental health, parent-child relationships and factors associated with the child's neighbourhood of residence (Duncan & Brooks-Gunn, 2000).

Recent research compares Canada with the US, UK and Australia, countries that have a largely market-based approach to child care (Bradbury, Corak, Waldfogel & Washbrook, 2012). When children are categorized into low, middle and high SES groupings, Canada has narrower gaps in cognitive/language and socio-emotional/behavioural outcomes at age 5 than do the US and the UK. However, a substantial gap in child abilities exists in each country by the time compulsory schooling starts—about one-third to one-half of a standard deviation gap between the bottom and middle on different measures of cognitive and language abilities. Smaller but consistent differences exist between children from low-SES and mid-SES backgrounds on behavioural indexes (hyperactivity/inattention and conduct).

SES gaps remain roughly constant over children's lifetimes (Bradbury, et al., 2012). However, in child health outcomes, differences based on SES cumulate as Canadian children age (Burton, Phipps & Zhang, 2013; Currie & Stabile, 2003; Currie et al., 2010; Stabile & Currie, 2007). Nearly half of children in the US who are born to low-income parents become low-income adults, whereas in Canada about one-third of such children become low-income adults (Corak, 2006). Ten years later, big gaps exist in high school completion and math scores between children who lived in poor vs. rich families when they were young. However, these gaps are bigger in the US than in Canada (Burton, Phipps & Zhang, 2013).

Some international studies find that the income-related inequality of outcomes among children is increasing over time (Corak, 2013a, 2013b; Duncan & Magnuson, 2011; Duncan & Murnane, 2011; OECD, 2011; Reardon, 2011). Others find that it is approximately constant (Blanden, Katz & Redmond, 2012). What seems clear is that the socioeconomic gradients are not diminishing over time.

Income inequality increased during the 1990s and 2000s, due largely to increased inequality in market incomes, and especially due to rapidly rising incomes in the top decile. At the top of the income distribution, rising incomes have not been accompanied by an increase in hours of paid work of family members. However, in the middle of the distribution, the stagnation of incomes has occurred despite significantly higher paid hours of work, especially by mothers. Thus, the growth of inequality has both an income and a time dimension for families with children (Burton & Phipps, 2011).

Child poverty is another marker that can give us a sense of whether there has been progress in raising family incomes for low-income families with children. Unfortunately, data problems and conceptual issues with measures of child poverty cloud the picture.

In their most recent report card, Campaign 2000 (2014) noted that the level of child poverty in 2012 was 19.1 percent in Canada, up from 15.8 percent in 1989, but down from 22.3 percent in 2000. The report uses the Low Income Measure (LIM), which is a measure of relative poverty, valuable for charting social exclusion and inequality. The LIM calculates the number of children whose families earn less than 50 percent of the median income after adjusting for family size.

The Vanier Institute (2010) reports that poverty among lone-mother families dropped from above 50 percent in the mid-1970s to less than 25 percent in 2007. Poverty among working-age couples with children has stayed nearly constant at about 5 percent. These calculations use the Low-Income Cut-Off (LICO). The LICO considers a family to be poor when it has an income level at which typical families of that size and in that size of urban area spend excessive amounts on food, clothing and shelter and are therefore likely to be unable to afford other necessities of life. However, the Low-Income Cut-Offs have not been re-calibrated since 1992.

Since Quebec's child care reforms were adopted in 1997, the rate of poverty among one-parent families with children under 5 years old dropped by 43 percent in that province, while poverty among young two-parent families dropped by 52 percent (Bouchard, 2013).

Considerable research evidence shows that early childhood education and care services can have particularly strong positive effects on children from disadvantaged and low-income backgrounds. In this context, it is somewhat puzzling that the recent expansion of early childhood education and care services in Canada has failed to narrow income-related gaps in child outcomes or to have substantial effects on child and family poverty outside Quebec.

## Do Disadvantaged Children Gain Access to ECEC Services in Canada?

Given that the employment of mothers and the use of regulated child care has continued to rise in Canada, it seems logical that the use of regulated child care by families from less-advantaged backgrounds should now be quite high. Let us see if that is true.

I define "disadvantaged families" as those in which the mother has a high school education or less. Are disadvantaged families likely to use regulated child care? Does child care act as a ramp into the paid labour force for mothers in these families, permitting them to earn higher incomes and their children to gain the benefits of higher-quality, licensed services? Given that there are child care subsidies in all provinces except Quebec targeted at families with relatively low incomes who are willing to work or study, we might expect positive answers to these questions.

Conventional wisdom suggests that a graph of the percentage of children using licensed child care against family income or education (that is, a line joining the tops of the bars in Figure 6.1 below) would have a U-shape, high at each end of the income scale and low in the middle. The argument is that families with low incomes are able to afford regulated child care because of the subsidy system while families with high incomes are able to afford licensed child care because they are affluent. This way of thinking leads us to believe that the affordability problem is concentrated in middle-income families who cannot afford the high costs of regulated child care.

The most recent Canada-wide data relevant to this subject come from Statistics Canada's 2010–11 Survey of Young Canadians (SYC). These data let us look at the use of licensed child care in Canada outside Quebec for children 1 year of age to school entry age, broken down by mother's education level (Figure 6.1). Even for employed or studying parents, when the mother has a high school education or less, only 24.5 percent use regulated child care, even though most should be eligible for provincial child care subsidies. When the mother has a college diploma or certificate and parents are employed or studying, 35.7 percent of children are in regulated care. For mothers with a bachelor's degree, the figure rises to 37.5 percent and for mothers with a post-graduate degree to 53.3 percent. In relation to mother's education, a graph of regulated child care use would not have a U-shape.

Even this description is a bit misleading, however, because it ignores the fact that, in Canada outside Quebec, only about half of mothers with a high school education or less having a child between 1 and 5 years of age are employed or studying. That compares to about 70 percent of mothers with a college certificate or diploma and about 75 percent of those with an undergraduate degree. Most families with a parent at home do not use non-parental child care.

The result is that children in the large majority of families in which mothers have a high school education or less do not gain access to the potential developmental benefits that regulated child care might have. Of the more than 340,000 children ages 1–5 with mothers having a high school education or less in Canada outside Quebec, only 15 percent are in regulated child care—this despite the fact that each province has a system of child care subsidies designed to encourage these mothers to be employed or receive training and to allow their children to gain access to the potential developmental benefits of regulated child care.

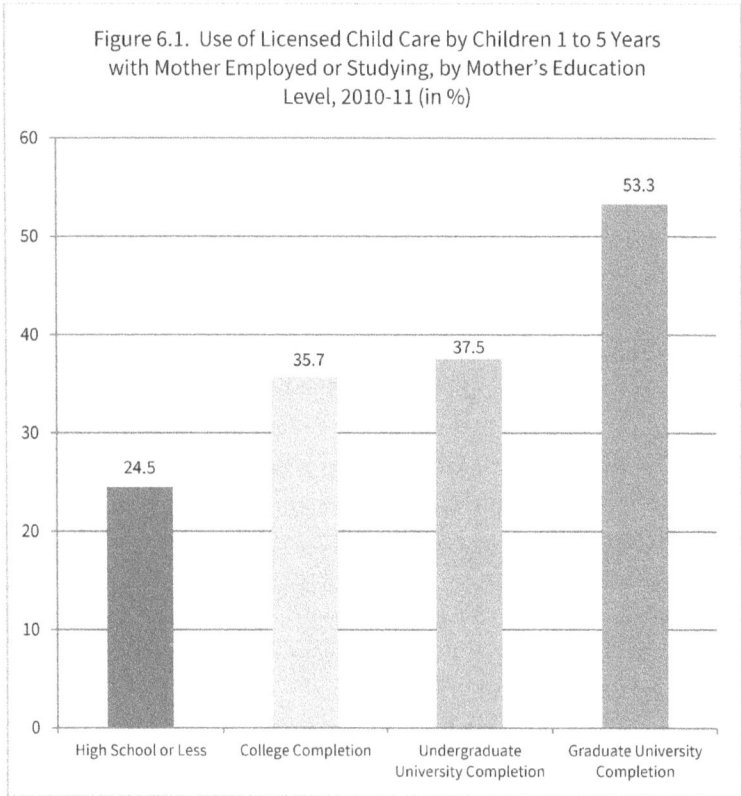

Figure 6.1. Use of Licensed Child Care by Children 1 to 5 Years with Mother Employed or Studying, by Mother's Education Level, 2010-11 (in %)

|  |  |
|---|---|
| High School or Less | 24.5 |
| College Completion | 35.7 |
| Undergraduate University Completion | 37.5 |
| Graduate University Completion | 53.3 |

Source: *Survey of Young Canadians, 2010-2011.*

How does this situation compare to Quebec, with its low cost, mainly publicly funded child care program? In Quebec, 61.8 percent of children 1–5 years with an employed or studying mother with a high school education or less use licensed child care. Including children with a mother who is not employed, 43.1 percent of Quebec children whose mother has a high school education or less are using licensed child care—about 30 percentage points higher than the comparable figure in the rest of Canada.

The evidence thus seems clear. The child care subsidy system in Canada outside Quebec is not achieving one of its chief goals. It does

Figure 6.2. Use of Licensed Child Care by Children 1 to 5 Years by Mother's Education Level, 2010-11 (in %)

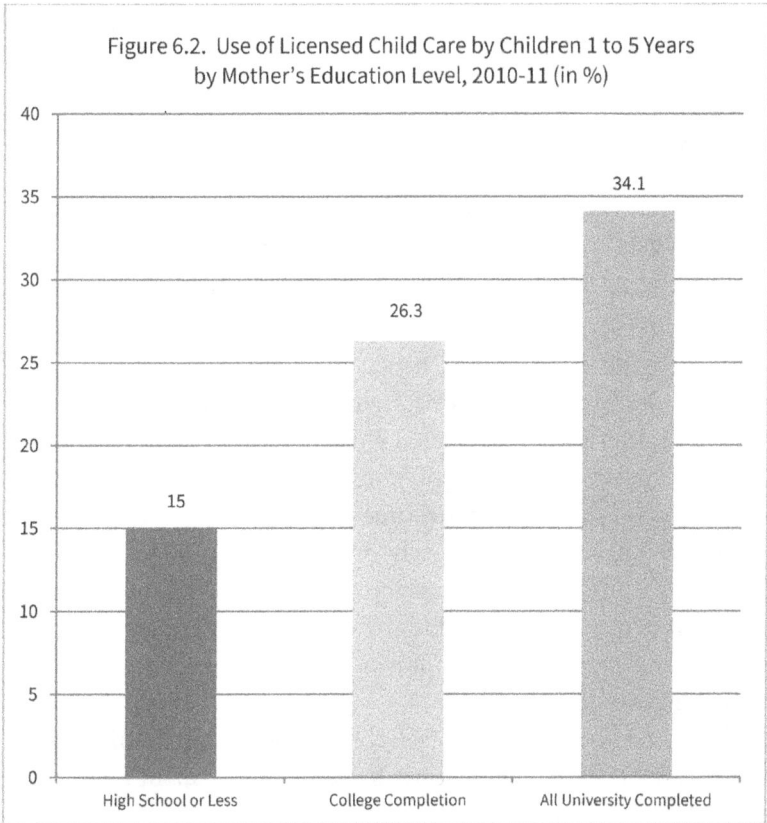

Source: *Survey of Young Canadians, 2010-2011.*

not provide persuasive incentives for mothers with a high school education or less to work and for their children to be exposed to potentially positive early childhood experiences. Therefore, apart from kindergarten attendance, most children who are likely to be disadvantaged do not gain access to ECEC services in Canada.

Can ECEC Policy Improve Mother's Employment and Family Incomes?
With colleagues, I have sought to measure the affordability of child care for families in Canada (Cleveland, Krashinsky & Forer, 2015). This work takes into account the market price of child care where families live and the number and age of their preschool children.

One of the measures is particularly relevant to the decisions families make about the use of regulated child care. It measures the net price of child care for the family (after taking into account child-care related benefits) as a percent of the after-tax contribution that the lower earner in the family is likely to be able to make to family income if she were employed in the paid labour force. The contribution of the lower earner is often smaller than one might think because of the income tax she must pay and the Employment Insurance and Canada Pension Plan contributions she must make, and also because her husband will lose the spousal benefit allowance that shelters some of his income from tax.

Focusing on two-parent families in Canada outside of Quebec, we find that regulated child care is not very affordable. Across all of the provinces excluding Quebec, just over half of the potential net contribution of the lower earner would, on average, go to paying the market cost of regulated child care. Is it then any wonder that a substantial number of mothers with preschool children remain out of the paid labour force and a substantial number who are in the paid labour force rely on care by parents or relatives? Because the loss of job experience tends to affect future earnings and employment positions, the effect of child care affordability on the earning capacity and employment prospects of women tends to be long-lasting.

There are good reasons to believe that improving the affordability of regulated child care would increase employment and labour market earnings for mothers, contributing to both gender equity and improving family incomes for low-income families with children. While some studies find that small cuts in the price of child care increase labour force participation only marginally, (Blau & Currie, 2006), the Quebec child care reforms beginning in the late 1990s provide evidence from a substantial reduction in the price of regulated child care and an increase in its supply. In 2002, the policy change increased the participation rate of mothers with at least one child 1 to 5 years of age by 8 percentage points (Lefebvre & Merrigan, 2005; 2008). Hours of work per year and weeks worked per year also increased. For mothers at all levels of education, the province's generous subsidization of day care had large, positive effects on labour supply and earnings (Lefebvre & Merrigan, 2008: 545).

What about the longer-term effects of Quebec's child care reforms? Did mothers who were encouraged to join the paid labour force by the availability of subsidized child care when their children were young stay in the paid labour force once their children reached school age? Before the child-care reforms, mothers with high school education or less and all children in school had an employment rate of only about 50 percent. However, when the reforms were phased in the employment rate of these mothers started to increase, reaching about 70 percent by 2002. This is a cohort for which attachment to the labour force is traditionally weak. The implication is that the child-care reforms had an important effect on families who are most at risk of being in poverty by encouraging mothers to join and stay in the labour force (Lefebvre, Merrigan & Verstraete, 2009).

The context for these dramatic increases is important. Employment rates for mothers with high school education or less started out low, so there was significant room for increase. The same long-term effects were not seen for mothers with higher levels of education because their pre-reform employment rates were already about 80 percent. A contributing factor to the increased long-term employment of mothers with high school education or less was the demand for labour. The late 1990s and early 2000s was a period of strong GDP growth in Quebec, so mothers could find jobs that were scarcer earlier.

Can Early Childhood Education and Care Reduce Child Outcome Gaps?
A considerable body of evidence shows that experience in early childhood education and care services can have positive effects on children's cognitive and language development and enduring positive effects on academic outcomes, completed education levels, employment and wages. These effects show up for ordinary full-day child care from early ages, for preschools and pre-kindergartens at about age 3 or 4, and for kindergartens at about age 5 (Ruhm & Waldfogel, 2011). However, the evidence is complex. Not every experience is positive. The magnitude of effects differs. Quality of care matters. What happens to parenting practices may matter.

And the size of the impact will depend on what type and quality of care the early childhood education and care services replace.

In considering the effects of early childhood education and care on reducing the socio-economic gradient in child outcomes, it is important to recognize that nearly every study finds that the effects on disadvantaged children are more strongly positive than for children who are less disadvantaged. These services do not need to be targeted interventions; ordinary ECEC programs, and particularly higher quality ECEC programs that are widely available to children, have also been found to narrow child outcome gaps.

QUALITY AND TYPE OF CARE. Generally speaking, the quality of ECEC is key to the magnitude of its effects on children's development. Thus, short-term effects on 4-year-old children in Tulsa, Oklahoma, prekindergarten programs were strongly related to the high quality of the services provided in the schools by teachers who had a teaching certificate and a certificate in early childhood education and who were paid at public school rates. Classroom size was capped at 20 and, with one lesser-trained assistant, this meant that staff-child ratios were 1:10 (Gormley, Gayer, Phillips & Dawson; 2005). In Danish centre-based child care, enduring improvement in cognitive effects was found to be related to differences in the average quality of care relative to the US. The results were especially strong for disadvantaged children, but were not maintained for disadvantaged children in the US (Esping Andersen et al., 2012). On average, family day care in Denmark is of worse quality than centre care. Looking at non-cognitive outcomes, one study found that family day care outcomes were significantly worse for boys whose mothers had lower levels of education than for other groups (Datta Gupta & Simonsen, 2010). Another study found that child-care subsidies that were not linked to the use of licensed services but were directed at low-income families in the US did little to encourage parents to use high-quality care, or even licensed care, but facilitated parental employment. For families receiving subsidies, negative developmental effects on children that endure through kindergarten were observed (Herbst & Tekin, 2010).

EFFECTS ON PARENTING. When studies find negative effects of ECEC, they can sometimes be traced to changes in child-rearing behaviours of parents after child care arrangements change. For instance, a US study found poorer interactions between parents and their children when low-income families received child care subsidies (Herbst & Tekin, 2014). Similarly, the rapid increase in the use of child care in Quebec had negative effects for some families and some children. In general, boys were worse off along several behavioral dimensions ranging from anxiety to hyperactivity and inattention because of changes in parental behaviour that were specific to boys (Kottelenberg & Lehrer, 2013c). A study of public preschool programs for 4-year-olds in the US found positive effects for children from low-income families on the amount of time that mothers spent reading with their children, on mothers' employment and on test scores of children through to eighth grade (Cascio & Schanzenbach, 2013).

CHARACTERISTICS OF LATER SCHOOLING/CARE. The positive effects of Head Start programs on children's development appear to fade more quickly for black children than white children in the US. The main reason seems to be that black children typically attend poorer quality schools once compulsory schooling starts (Currie & Thomas, 2000). A US study found superior reading and math skills for children attending prekindergarten. Superiority did not persist in small, high-instruction classrooms because, in that environment, other children were able to catch up. However, in large, low-instruction classrooms, the preschool advantage persisted because of the low performance of children who were previously cared for exclusively by parents (Magnuson, Ruhm & Waldfogel, 2007b). It thus seems that the longer-term effects of early childhood experience depend partly on classroom experience during at least the first years of school.

THE QUALITY OF CARE THAT IS REPLACED. The replacement of one type of care by another is a major factor explaining why developmental effects on low-income children are nearly always more positive than they are for higher-income children. For low-income children, access to centre-based ECEC of reasonable quality typically replaces care by a relative, neighbour or parent. Consequently, research shows that all children usually benefit from kindergarten in the United States, but Hispanic children, non-English speakers, children from immigrant households, and children of low socioeconomic status benefit most (Dhuey, 2011). However, if, before the introduction of universal kindergarten, black children from low-income families are already attending ECEC of relatively good quality, such as Head Start, while white children do not have access to regulated ECEC, a universal program may make black children worse off than white children in terms of long-term positive effects on high school dropout rates and institutionalization rates (Cancio, 2009).

SOCIOEMOTIONAL/BEHAVIOURAL EFFECTS. Intensive early intervention projects have strong cognitive, language and socio-emotional or behavioural benefits for children. Some researchers have argued that the latter are especially important. In particular, advances in the ability to concentrate, improvements in the emotional disposition to share and co-operate, reductions in aggressive behavioural tendencies and progress in the ability to self-regulate begin a virtuous cycle of learning (Heckman, 2007; Heckman et al., 2006; Heckman & Mosso, 2014; Cunha & Heckman, 2009).

However, researchers have also suggested that child care, particularly when it is of less than adequate quality, can have negative effects on non-cognitive traits. For instance, some US studies have found that better quality child care is associated with better socio-emotional and peer outcomes at some ages—but more child care hours over the child's life predict more behaviour problems and conflict as reported by care providers. And although more time in centre-based care is related to higher cognitive and language scores, it is also related to more problem behaviours and fewer prosocial behaviours as reported by care providers (NICHD-EC-CRN, 2006). Significantly, however, program quality moderates behaviour problems; high-quality pre-kindergartens in public schools does not have adverse behavioural impacts (Magnuson, Ruhm & Waldfogel, 2007a).

A pattern of negative socio-emotional and behavioural effects of regulated child care has also been found in Quebec (Baker, Gruber & Milligan, 2008). The universal child-care initiative in that province dramatically increased the use of regulated child care over time and had strong positive effects on maternal labour supply. However, on socio-emotional measures such as aggression and hyperactivitiy/inattention, children in Quebec did worse than similar children in the rest of Canada over the same period. The rapid expansion of low-quality family day care was likely largely responsible for these negative effects (Ruhm & Waldfogel, 2011).

The Quebec data were later re-analyzed to determine the origins of the negative effects (Kottelenberg & Lehrer, 2013a, 2013b, 2013c). The researchers found that the negative effects were concentrated in children who began child care at a very young age. Positive effects on motor and social development were found for 3-year-olds. There was no evidence of negative developmental effects for 3- and 4-year-olds. Moreover, negative socio-emotional and behavioural effects were discovered only for boys. They appear to have been fostered at least partially by changes in parenting practices and home environments, such as decreasing the amount of time spent reading with children once the child was enrolled in child care. The researchers also found positive effects on behaviours for the most disadvantaged children (Kottelenberg & Lehrer, 2013b).

A companion analysis found the average effect of child care across Canada including Quebec is positive for motor and social development but is not significantly negative for any socio-emotional or behavioural indicator (Kottelenberg and Lehrer, 2013a). These results make it clear that when it comes to assessing the impacts of early childhood education and care services on children, the details matter enormously. Positive and negative effects are both possible, and a mix of the two is perhaps likely, depending on quality and type of care, child and family background, gender, child age and the impact of new programs on parenting behaviours.

In sum, there are good reasons to believe that some forms of centre-based child care, preschool, and prekindergarten can have important positive effects on children, whether these children are disadvantaged and low-income and from single-parent families or are from middle-income and two-parent families. Effect sizes appear to depend on the quality and type of child care/early education they receive and the support and stimulation the children would have alternatively received (often related to the family situation of the child) if they had not been enrolled in such a program. The age and perhaps the gender of the child moderate both of these factors, and the persistence of improved child outcomes depends on later classroom experiences.

## How Does Policy Need to Change to Produce More Equitable Results?

It seems clear from the foregoing analysis that early childhood education and care is capable of improving child, family and gender equity. However, current Canadian policies are not achieving their potential. Seven policy reforms and behavioural changes could help in this regard:

1. Child care needs to be more affordable. Cost continues to be an important barrier to full labour force participation, especially for women whose earnings are low because of education/training, immigrant status, First Nations status, ethnic background or other factors.

2. The weak position of mothers in the labour force is a consequence of the fact that they nearly always have primary responsibility for child rearing and for making the labour force adjustments that child rearing requires. If this burden were more equally shared between men and women, mothers would not face the same forms and degree of discrimination they now do and employment situations would have to adjust for the expectation that all parents spend time and energy caring for children. Schools, day care centres, and all of society's institutions need to encourage more fathers to take much more responsibility for child rearing.

3. Increasing the amount of available full-time parental leave is probably not as advantageous as many people think. Recent research has found that, since mothers take the large majority of parental leave, extensions beyond current amounts of leave are likely to have negative effects on mothers' wages. One way to encourage the participation of both parents in child rearing is for the rest of Canada to follow Quebec and Western Europe in introducing "daddy weeks" in parental leave arrangements. Daddy weeks are reserved for the parent who does not take the bulk of parental leave, usually the father. Daddy leave is available on a "use-it-or-lose-it" basis; it is not compulsory that fathers take it but the weeks are not transferable. In Quebec and Western Europe, this policy has been quite successful in getting fathers to take more responsibility for child care. It is, however, worth investigating whether Swedish policies that permit parents to work just six hours a day in the early years of a child's life have positive effects on children while avoiding negative effects on mother's earnings. In general,

policies should be designed so that the typical child-care day is not too long, especially for very young children.

4. Child care subsidy arrangements in most of Canada are designed to encourage low-income families, especially single parents, to seek employment or training and to give their children access to good quality ECEC services. They do not appear to be working well. Outside Quebec, only about 15 percent of children in families where the mother has a high school education or less use regulated child care. Quebec's child care policy, offering universal, low-fee, regulated child care, appears to be much more successful in encouraging mothers with low levels of education to use child care and gain employment in the paid labour force. Low fees need to be transparent and certain and not associated with low-income stigma if they are to be the basis of changed employment behaviours.

5. Quebec can also teach the rest of Canada lessons by negative example. First, when major new early childhood education and care programs are rolled out, it is important to ensure that they are of disproportionate benefit to families that are disadvantaged. A policy that focuses on lowering current child care prices will initially benefit families currently using regulated child care, especially those that are in the middle and upper ranges of the income distribution. Without special measures, those who need assistance most are least likely to receive it.

6. Quebec's experience can also teach the rest of Canada that it is difficult to maintain and improve child care quality when an early childhood education and care system is expanded rapidly. The quality of child care service in Quebec is inadequate. Non-profit, entirely government-subsidized early childhood centres are typically of good quality but there are not enough spaces in them to meet demand. The quality of for-profit centres is problematic (Cleveland & Bigras, 2013). Subsidized family day care has filled many of the supply needs of a rapidly growing ECEC system in Quebec, and is conveniently available especially in small cities, towns and rural areas. However, the amount of early childhood training and knowledge of family day care providers is minimal; most studies of quality in subsidized family day care find that it is not of the educational quality that the Quebec system anticipates.

My advice to the rest of Canada is to build out new ECEC systems more slowly but build them with good quality services that will serve as the foundation of a system that will last and that parents and governments will celebrate.

7. Parenting and good quality early childhood education and care services need to complement each other in fostering children's development. If ECEC reforms are paired with reduced interest in, and attention to, parenting, the positive effects of ECEC will be moderated or nullified. If ECEC reforms stimulate an active partnership between parents and child care teachers, their positive effects will be multiplied. Early childhood services need to pay attention to parent involvement and they need to encourage positive parenting.

Based on the research reviewed here, it seems safe to conclude that the types of policies I have outlined are likely to enhance the contribution that early childhood education and care make to gender, child and family equality in Canada.

## References

Abella, R. S. 1984. *Equality in Employment: A Royal Commission Report. Royal Commission on Equality in Employment.* Ottawa: Minister of Supply and Services, Canada.

Baker, M., J. Gruber & K. Milligan. 2008. "Universal childcare, maternal labor supply and family well-being." *Journal of Political Economy*, 79, pp. 709–45.

Blanden, J., I. Katz & G. Redmond. 2012. "Family background and child outcomes." In *From Parents to Children: The Intergenerational Transmission of Advantage.* J. Ermisch, M. Jantti & T. M. Smeeding (Eds.), New York: Russell Sage Foundation.

Blau, D.M. & J. Currie. 2006. "Who's minding the kids? Preschool, day care, and after school care." In *The Handbook Of The Economics Of Education.* E. Hanushek and F. Welch (Eds.), New York: Elsevier/North-Holland, pp. 1116–1278.

Bouchard, C. 2013. "Early intervention national policy: Successes and pitfalls." Presentation at 15th International Congress of the AIFREF, Patras, Greece.

Bradbury, B., M. Corak, J. Waldfogel & E. Washbrook. 2012. "Inequality in early childhood outcomes." J. Ermisch, M. Jantti and T. M. Smeeding (Eds.), *From Parents to Children: The Intergenerational Transmission of Advantage.* New York: Russell Sage Foundation.

Bradley, R. H. & R. F. Corwyn. 2002. "Socioeconomic status and child development." *Annual Review Of Psychology*, 53, pp. 371–99.

Burton, P. & S. Phipps. 2011. "Families, time and well-being in Canada." *Canadian Public Policy*, 37, 3, pp. 395–423.

Burton, P., S. Phipps & L. Zhang. 2013. "From parent to child: emerging inequality in outcomes for children in Canada and the U.S." *Child Indicators Research*, 6, pp. 363–400.

Campaign 2000. 2014. *2014 Report Card on Child and Family Poverty in Canada.* Toronto: Family Services Toronto.

Cascio, E. 2009. "Maternal labor supply and the introduction of kindergartens into American public schools." *Journal of Human Resources*, 44, pp. 140-170.

Cascio, E., & D. Schanzenbach. 2013. "The impacts of expanding access to high-quality preschool education." Working Paper 19735. New York: National Bureau of Economic Research.

Cleveland, G. 2012. "The economics of early childhood education and care in Canada." In *Recent Perspectives on Early Childhood Education in Canada*, N. Howe and L. Prochner (eds.) Toronto: University of Toronto Press, Scholarly Publishing Division. Chapter 3, pp. 80–108.

Cleveland, G. 2015. "ECEC policy in Canada: Availability, affordability and quality." *Our Schools, Our Selves*, 244, pp. 107–121.

Cleveland, G., B. Forer, D. Hyatt, C. Japel & M. Krashinsky. 2008. "New evidence about child care in Canada: Use patterns, affordability and quality." *IRPP Choices*, 14, 12, pp. 2–42.

Cleveland, G. and B. Forer. 2010. "Child care use and child development in immigrant, lone mother, rural and official language minority families in Canada." Working Paper. http://www.childcarepolicy.net/publications/.

Cleveland, G., M. Krashinsky & B. Forer. 2015. "Assessing the affordability of regulated child care in Canada." Working Paper. University of Toronto Scarborough.

Cleveland, G. & N. Bigras. 2013. "The Determinants of Child Care Quality in Quebec: How Specification Matters." Working Paper. University of Toronto Scarborough.

Conti, G. & J. J. Heckman. 2012. "The economics of child well-being." NBER Working Paper No. 18466. New York: National Bureau of Economic Research.

Corak, M. 2013a. "Income inequality, equality of opportunity, and intergenerational mobility." *Journal of Economic Perspectives*, 27, 3, pp. 79–102.

Corak, M. 2006. "Do poor children become poor adults? Lessons from a cross country comparison of generational earnings mobility." *Research on Economic Inequality*, 131, pp. 143–88.

Corak, M. 2013b. "Inequality from generation to generation: The United States in comparison." In *The Economics of Inequality, Poverty, and Discrimination in the 21st Century*. R. S. Rycroft (Ed.) Santa Barbara, CA: ABC-CLIO.

Cunha, F. & J. J. Heckman. 2009. "The economics and psychology of inequality and human development." *Journal of the European Economic Association*, 7, 2, pp. 320–64.

Currie, J. & D. Thomas. 2000. "School quality and the longer-term effects of Head Start." *Journal of Human Resources*, 35, 4, pp. 755–74.

Currie, J. & M. Stabile. 2003. "Socioeconomic status and child health: why is the relationship stronger for older children?" *American Economic Review*, 93, pp. 1813–1823.

Currie, J., M. Stabile, P. Manivong & L. Roos. 2010. "Child health and young adult outcomes." *Journal of Human Resources*, 45, 3, pp. 517–48.

Datta Gupta, N. & M. Simonsen. 2010. "Non-cognitive child outcomes and universal high-quality child care." *Journal of Public Economics* 941-2: 30–43.

Dhuey, E. 2011. "Who benefits from kindergarten? Evidence from the introduction of state subsidization." *Education Evaluation and Policy Analysis*, 33, 1, pp. 3–22.

Duncan, G. & J. Brooks-Gunn. 2000. "Family poverty, welfare reform, and child development." *Child Development*, 71, 1, 188–96.

Duncan, G., and R. Murnane. (Eds.) 2011. *Whither Opportunity: Rising Inequality, Schools, and Children's Life Chances*. New York: Russell Sage Foundation.

Duncan, G. J. & K. Magnuson. 2011. "The nature and impact of early achievement skills, attention skills, and behavior problems." In *Whither Opportunity: Rising Inequality, Schools, and Children's Life Chances*. G. J. Duncan and R. Murnane (Eds.). New York: Russell Sage Foundation.

Duncan, G. J., K. M. Ziol-Guest & A. Kalil. 2010. "Early-childhood poverty and adult attainment, behavior, and health." *Child Development*, 81, 1, pp. 306–25.

Esping-Andersen, G., I. Garfinkel, W-J. Han, K. Magnuson, S. Wagner & J. Waldfogel. 2012. "Child care and school performance in Denmark and the United States." *Children and Youth Services Review*, 34, pp. 576–89.

Fortin, N. & T. Schirle. 2007. "Gender dimensions of changes in earnings inequality in Canada." In *Dimensions of Inequality in Canada*. D. Green & J.R. Kesselman (eds.). Vancouver, B.C.: UBC Press. Chapter 11.

Friendly, M., S. Halfon, J. Beach & B. Forer. 2013. *Early Childhood Education and Care in Canada 2012*. Toronto: Childcare Resource and Research Unit.

Gormley, W.T. Jr., T. Gayer, D. Phillips & B. Dawson. 2005. "The effects of universal Pre-K on cognitive development." *Developmental Psychology*, 41, pp. 872–84.

Heckman, J. 2007. "The economics, technology and neuroscience of human capability formation." Working Paper No. 13195. New York: National Bureau of Economic Research.

Heckman, J., J. Stixrud & S. Urzua. 2006. "The effects of cognitive and noncognitive abilities on labor market outcomes and social behavior." *Journal of Labor Economics*, 24, 411–82.

Heckman, J. & S. Mosso. 2014. "The economics of human development and social mobility." Working Paper No. 19925. New York: National Bureau of Economic Research.

Herbst, C. & E. Tekin. 2010. "Child care subsidies and child development." *Economics of Education Review* 29, pp. 618–38.

Herbst, C. & E. Tekin. 2014. "Child care subsidies, maternal health, and child-parent interactions: evidence from three nationally representative datasets." *Health Economics*, 23, pp. 894–916.

Kottelenberg, M. & S. Lehrer. 2013a. "New evidence on the impacts of access to and attending universal child-care in Canada." *Canadian Public Policy*, 39, 2, pp. 263–85.

Kottelenberg, M. & S. Lehrer. 2013b. "Do the perils of universal child care depend on the child's age?" Working Paper No. 132. Canadian Labour Market and Skills Researcher Network.

Kottelenberg, M. & S. Lehrer. 2013c. "The gender effects of universal child care in Canada: Much ado about boys?" Working Paper. Queen's University.

Lefebvre, P. & P. Merrigan. 2005. "Low-fee ($5/day/child) regulated childcare policy and the labor supply of mothers with young children: A natural experiment from Canada." Working Paper 05-08. Inter-university Centre on Risk, Economic Policies and Employment (CIRPÉE).

Lefebvre P. & P. Merrigan. 2008. "Child-care policy and the labor supply of mothers with young children: A natural experiment from Canada." *Journal of Labor Economics*, 26, pp. 519–48.

Lefebvre P., P. Merrigan & M. Verstraete. 2009. "Dynamic labour supply effects of childcare subsidies: Evidence from a Canadian natural experiment on low-fee universal child care." *Labour Economics*, 16, pp. 490–502.

Magnuson, K.A., C. Ruhm & J. Waldfogel. 2007a. "Does pre-kindergarten improve school preparation and performance?" *Economics of Education Review*, 26, pp. 33–51.

Magnuson, K.A., C. Ruhm & J. Waldfogel. 2007b. "The persistence of preschool effects: Do subsequent classroom experiences matter?" *Early Childhood Research Quarterly*, 22, pp. 18–38.

NICHD-ECCRN (National Institute of Child Health and Human Development Early Child Care Research Network). 2006. "Child-Care effect sizes for the NICHD Study of Early Child Care and Youth Development." *American Psychologist*, 61, 2, pp. 99–116.

Nicholson, J. M., N. Lucas, D. Berthelsen & M. Wake. 2012. "Socioeconomic inequality profiles in physical and developmental health from 0-7 years: Australian National Study." *Journal of Epidemiology and Community Health*, 66, 1, pp. 81–7.

OECD (Organisation for Economic Co-operation and Development). 2011. *Divided We Stand: Why Inequality Keeps Rising*. Paris: OECD Publishing.

Phipps, S., P. Burton & L. Lethbridge. 2001. "In and out of the labour market: long-term income consequences of child-related interruptions to women's paid work." *Canadian Journal of Economics*, 34, 2, pp. 411–29.

Reardon, S. F. 2011. "The widening academic achievement gap between the rich and the poor: new evidence and possible explanations." In *Whither Opportunity? Rising Inequality, Schools, and Children's Life Chances*. G. J. Duncan & R. J. Murnane (Eds.), New York: Russell Sage Foundation.

Ruhm, C., and J. Waldfogel. 2011. "Long-term effects of early childhood care and education." IZA DP No. 6149. Discussion Paper Series. Bonn, Germany: Institute for the Study of Labor.

Stabile, M. & J. Currie. 2007. "Mental health in childhood and human capital." Working Paper 13217, New York: National Bureau of Economic Research.

TD Economics. 2007. "Market forces advance prospects for women in the workforce: TD Economics" http://www.td.com/document/PDF/economics/special/td-economics-special-bc0907-woman-pr.pdf.

Vanier Institute of the Family. 2010. *Families Count: Profiling Canada's Families.* Ottawa: Vanier Institute of the Family.

Vincent, C. 2013. "Why do women earn less than men? A synthesis of findings from Canadian microdata." CRDCN Synthesis Series, Canadian Research Data Centre Network.

Waldfogel, J. 1998. "Understanding the 'family gap' in pay for women with children." *Journal of Economic Perspectives.* 12, 1, pp. 137–56.

Waldfogel, J. & I. Pal. 2014. "Re-visiting the family gap in pay in the United States." Working Paper, Columbia University.

Zhang, X. 2008. "The post-childbirth employment of Canadian mothers and the earnings trajectories of their continuously employed counterparts, 1983 to 2004." Analytical Studies Branch Research Paper Series, Statistics Canada catalogue no. 11F00119M.

CHAPTER SEVEN

# Gender Equality and the Role of Power, Politics and Representation

Emily Laxer

## Introduction

The chapters by Ito Peng and Gordon Cleveland raise two key questions regarding the relationship between welfare policy and gender equality. First, which policy features of modern welfare states affect women and families? Second, how do these policies contribute to or detract from gender equality in the spheres of paid work and the household? Peng identifies multiple mechanisms by which countries' distinct welfare models influence women's positions in the labour force, emphasizing that those residing in social-democratic countries enjoy the highest levels of equality in work and pay. She further observes that new social and economic contexts are giving rise to income disparities among women, depending on their race, ethnicity and immigration experiences. Cleveland fills in the narrative by analyzing childcare policy and its implications for gender equality in Canada. He presents strong evidence that affordable, widely available, and high quality childcare not only improves the lives of children; it also significantly increases the likelihood that mothers will enter the paid labour force.

I propose that, in answering Peng's call to consider emerging disparities among women of different racial, ethnic and immigration backgrounds, scholars should pay attention to how these disparities relate to control or lack of control over the levers of state power. More than mere conduits of public opinion, political parties play a key role in constituting and articulating the public's interest with regard to social welfare policy. Reducing inter- and intra-gender inequality is thus a political project, and one that will require significant improvement in representation by women and racialized political candidates.

### Gender Inequality and the Welfare State: The Role of Intra-Gender Disparities

Whereas the gendered dimensions of welfare policy are now well understood (Lewis, 1992; O'Connor, 1996; Orloff, 1993), processes of racial and immigrant exclusion remain understudied in the welfare state literature. This is the case despite evidence that the institutions governing integration into the paid labour force have both a gendered and a racial dimension, with racialized immigrant women overrepresented in the most precarious, low-income positions in the Canadian labour market (Chui & Maheux, 2011). Canada's immigrant selection process contributes significantly to this outcome. Since the late 1960s, the country's immigration system has put a premium on education and work experience as eligibility criteria (Citizenship and Immigration Canada, n.d.). Yet evidence shows that immigrants' credentials often go unrecognized and that few mechanisms exist to facilitate certification of foreign credentials and skill upgrades (Boyd & Thomas, 2001; Reitz, 2001).

The problem of skill underutilization is especially marked for female immigrants to Canada, particularly the highly educated (Beach & Worswick, 1993). This is partly due to gender differences in pathways to citizenship. Because women are more likely than men are to enter Canada under the family class of immigrants (Chui, 2011), they are also more susceptible than their male counterparts to the social and financial dependence caused by delays in obtaining permanent residency (Goldring, Berinstein & Bernhard, 2009). These effects are particularly concerning given evidence that uncertainty in status produces job precariousness long after status is obtained (Goldring & Landolt, 2011).

The trend toward temporary migration exacerbates the challenges that Canada's female immigrants face. To fill labour shortages, the federal government has issued hundreds of thousands of temporary work permits, with the result that a growing number of Canada's workers currently lack full resident, citizenship and labour rights (Goldring et al., 2009: 247; Lenard & Straehle, 2012). Female temporary foreign workers face unique hurdles. Consider domestic caregivers arriving under the Live-in Caregiver Program. Primarily recruited from the Philippines, a good number of these caregivers hold university or nursing degrees. Yet their earnings and working conditions are not commensurate with their skills (Brickner & Straehle, 2010; Langevin & Belleau, 2000). Moreover, although Stephen Harper's Conservative government dropped the program's live-in requirement, participants' prospects for citizenship continue to depend on their highly unequal relationships to their employers (Langevin & Belleau, 2000).

The politicization of religious expression in public sector employment constitutes a third potential source of intra-gender inequality in Canada's workforce. Although the outcome of the 2015 federal election makes legislative change unlikely in the near future, the highly charged niqab issue has gained prominence, especially in Quebec. Campaigns to restrict the niqab and other religious symbols in civil service employment reinforce anti-Islamic prejudice, thus erecting new obstacles to Muslim women's full and equal participation in the labour force.

Racialized immigrant women thus face a triple disadvantage in Canada's paid labour force. As women, they are subject to wide-ranging barriers to equal pay with men. As racialized individuals, they face discrimination on the basis of their origins, culture and religion. As immigrants, they are vulnerable to the lasting effects of status precariousness. As I will now argue, addressing these disadvantages is in part a political project, one that will require significant overhaul of the structures of power, politics and representation in Canada.

### Addressing Inter- and Intra-Gender Disparities in Welfare: A Political Project

Peng rightly emphasizes that welfare state policies are outcomes of conflicts that are contested by political parties. As such, parties play a critical role in shaping the tenor of debate around welfare policies and their gendered implications.

Consider the debates surrounding child care provision in Canada's 2015 federal election campaign. Despite evidence that initiatives to trim state expenditures benefit mainly middle- and upper-level income earners, the Conservative and Liberal parties continued to advocate child care as a market service based on choice. The Conservative Party urged a continuation of its family tax credits, spousal income splitting and child care expense deductions (Conservative Party of Canada, 2015). The Liberal platform was more generous but no less individualized (Liberal Party of Canada, 2015). Only the New Democratic Party (NDP) underscored the link between child care and women's participation in the paid labour force, which it proposed to address through a universal, affordable child care policy modelled on Quebec's program (New Democratic Party, 2014). By framing the childcare issue as affecting individual families rather than society as a whole, none of the leading parties directly addressed the underlying systems of inequality that prevent certain women from receiving the full benefits of any of these policies.

How can this situation be ameliorated? How can the triple disadvantage that racialized and immigrant women encounter in Canada's paid labour force be made a policy priority? A crucial step is to focus on reducing the democratic deficit that results from women's—particularly minority women's—under-representation in Canadian politics. Indeed, although the proportion of women candidates in Canadian elections has increased (Carbert, 2012), it differs markedly across parties, with the federal NDP ahead of its competitors in 2015 (Anderssen, 2015). Moreover, although the number of female parliamentarians reached a record high 26 percent in 2015 (Shendruk & Taylor-Vaisey, 2015), growth in representation has plateaued in Canada over the last two decades (Bashevkin, 2011). The underrepresentation of visible minority women is acute. Although Canadians elected a record 46 visible-minority MPs on October 19th, 2015, only 15 are women (Shendruk & Taylor-Vaisey, 2015). As such, visible minority women make up 4.5 percent of Parliament, less than half their proportion in the Canadian population as a whole.

The United Nations has determined that, in order to see a marked shift toward policies that benefit women, the proportion of female representatives must reach a critical mass of 30 percent (UN Women, 2015). A number of mechanisms have been proposed to reach this target in Canada. For example, laws can be passed that allow candidates to take unpaid leave from their jobs to contest nominations and elections; set spending limits for nomination and election campaigns; make contributions for nomination campaigns tax deductible; treat child care and housekeeping costs as reimbursable campaign expenses; and so on. Additionally, laws can be enacted that make government subsidies to political party campaigns dependent on the proportion of parties' elected candidates who are women (Bashevkin, 2009; Brodie, 1991). Improving the representation of visible minority women in particular will require more far-reaching changes, including a much stronger commitment to reducing the barriers to citizenship that many in this group face.

## Conclusion

Feminists have long recognized that reducing gender inequality in the work and domestic spheres requires increased control of state power by people who wish to transform the gendered assumptions of citizenship. Following his October 2015 election victory, Prime Minister Justin Trudeau appointed a cabinet that features an equal number of male and female ministers (although most of the women hold junior portfolios). This is an important step forward. However, to see lasting improvement in inter- and intra-gender inequality in Canada, we must address the underrepresentation of racialized and immigrant women in politics generally and work to ensure that those with an equality agenda have the opportunity to shape the policy landscape.

## References

Anderssen, E. (2015, October 20). Federal Election 2015: We Have a Record Number of Female MPs, but Hold the Applause. *Globe & Mail.*

Bashevkin, S. (2009). *Women, Power, Politics.* Toronto: Oxford University Press.

Bashevkin, S. (2011). Women's Representation in the House of Commons: A Stalemate? *Canadian Parliamentary Review,* Spring, 17–22.

Beach, C. M., & Worswick, C. (1993). Is There a Double-Negative Effect on the Earnings of Immigrant Women? *Canadian Public Policy,* 19(1), 36–53.

Boyd, M., & Thomas, D. (2001). Match or Mismatch? The Employment of Immigrant Engineers in Canada's Labor Force. *Population Research and Policy Review,* 20(1/2), 107–133.

Brickner, R. K., & Straehle, C. (2010). The missing link: Gender, immigration policy and the Live-in Caregiver Program in Canada. *Policy and Society,* 29, 309–320.

Brodie, J. (1991). Women and the Electoral Process in Canada. In K. Megyery (Ed.), *Women in Canadian Politics: Toward Equity in Representation.* Toronto: Dundurn Press.

Carbert, L. (2012). The Hidden Rise of New Women Candidates Seeking Election to the House of Commons, 2000–2008. *Canadian Political Science Review,* 6(2–3), 143–157.

Chui, T. (2011). *Immigrant Women (Women in Canada: A Gender-based Statistical Report).* Ottawa: Statistics Canada, Social and Aboriginal Statistics Division.

Chui, T., & Maheux, H. (2011). *Visible Minority Women (Women in Canada: A Gender-based Statistical Report No. 89-503-x).* Statistics Canada.

Citizenship and Immigration Canada. (n.d.). Six Selection Factors—Federal Skilled Workers. http://www.cic.gc.ca/english/immigrate/skilled/apply-factors.asp.

Conservative Party of Canada. (2015). *Supporting Families.* http://www.conservative.ca/where-we-stand/supporting-families/.

Goldring, L., Berinstein, C., & Bernhard, J. K. (2009). Institutionalizing Precarious Migratory Status in Canada. *Citizenship Studies,* 13(3), 239–265.

Goldring, L., & Landolt, P. (2011). Caught in the Work-Citizenship Matrix: the Lasting Effects of Precarious Legal Status on Work for Toronto Immigrants. *Globalizations,* 8(3), 325–341.

Langevin, L., & Belleau, M.-C. (2000). *Trafficking in Women in Canada: A Critical Analysis of the Legal Framework Governing Immigrant Live-in Caregivers and Mail-Order Brides.* Status of Women Canada. http://www.childtrafficking.com/Docs/langevin_2000__trafficking_.pdf.

Lenard, P. T., & Straehle, C. (Eds.). (2012). *Legislated Inequality: Temporary Labour Migration in Canada.* Montreal: McGill-Queen's University Press.

Lewis, J. (1992). Gender and the Development of Welfare Regimes. *Journal of European Social Policy,* 2(3), 159–173.

Liberal Party of Canada. (2015). *Justin Trudeau's Plan for Fairness for the Middle Class.* https://www.liberal.ca/files/2015/05/Fairness-for-the-Middle-Class.pdf.

New Democratic Party. (2014). *Tom Mulcair's Affordable Childcare Plan.* http://www.ndp.ca/childcare.

O'Connor, J. S. (1996). Understanding Women in Welfare States. *Current Sociology,* 44(2), 1–12.

Orloff, A. S. (1993). Gender and the Social Rights of Citizenship: The Comparative Analysis of Gender Relations and Welfare States. *American Sociological Review,* 58, 303–328.

Reitz, J. G. (2001). Immigrant Skill Utilization in the Canadian Labour Market: Implications of Human Capital Research. *Journal of International Migration and Integration,* 2(3), 347–378.

Shendruk, A., & Taylor-Vaisey, N. (2015, October 20). The Shape of the House: An Interactive Exploration of the 42nd Parliament. *Maclean's.*

UN Women. (2015, December). *Facts and Figures: Leadership and Political Participation.* http://www.unwomen.org/en/what-we-do/leadership-and-political-participation/facts-and-figures.

# About the Authors

*Robert Andersen* is Dean of Social Science, Western University, London, Ontario. The author of numerous awards for his publications, he studies the effects of economic inequality on attitudes and political actions. His most recent research examines the interaction between national-level income inequality and individual-level economic position (as measured by social class or income) in their effects on various outcomes such as attitudes toward income inequality, social tolerance, support for capitalist ideology and civic participation.

*Robert Brym* is S.D. Clark Professor of Sociology in the Department of Sociology, University of Toronto, and a Fellow of the Royal Society of Canada. He has published widely on politics in Canada, Russia, and Israel/Palestine. The winner of numerous awards for his teaching and scholarly work, his writings have been translated into nine languages. His recent research projects focus on collective and state violence in Israel and Palestine; democracy and intolerance in the Middle East and North Africa; and student protest in Toronto and Montreal.

*Gordon Cleveland* is an economist in the Department of Management at the University of Toronto Scarborough, and has recently been Honorary Senior Fellow at the Graduate School of Education, University of Melbourne. He is collaborating investigator with a research team of educators and psychologists at the University of Quebec at Montreal and Laval University studying early education and child care services in Quebec. With co-authors, he has studied many aspects of economic and policy issues relevant to early childhood education and care. His most recent work focuses on measuring the affordability and use patterns of child care services and on econometric techniques used to uncover causal patterns in early childhood research.

*Emily Laxer* recently received her PhD in Sociology at the University of Toronto. Supported by the Social Sciences and Humanities Research Council, her dissertation research examines the role of political party conflict in producing laws that restrict Islamic veiling in France. She has also published on nation building in Quebec's reasonable accommodation debate and on immigrant voting and civic engagement in Canada. She is now a postdoctoral fellow at the University of Michigan, Ann Arbor, funded by the Social Sciences and Humanities Research Council.

*John Myles* is Emeritus Professor of Sociology and Senior Fellow in the School of Public Policy and Governance, University of Toronto. Until 2012, he was Canada Research Chair in the Social Foundations of Public Policy and, for many years, Senior Visiting Scholar at Statistics Canada. He has written widely on the comparative politics of the welfare state and on topics related to income inequality and poverty. His recent publications have focused on the politics of income redistribution in Canada. He is a Fellow of the Royal Society of Canada and holds an honorary doctorate from the University of Leuven (Belgium) for his contributions to old age security policy.

*Lars Osberg* is McCulloch Professor of Economics, Dalhousie University, Halifax, Nova Scotia. He has held visiting positions at Cambridge, New York University and the Universities of Sydney, New South Wales and Essex. He has also served as Senior Visiting Research Fellow at Research on Poverty Alleviation, Dar es Salaam; Visiting Scholar at the Indira Ghandi Institute for Development Research, Mumbai; and Visiting Consultant at the OECD in Paris. He is the author of many books, journal articles, and book chapters. His current research emphasizes the measurement and determinants of poverty and economic insecurity, the implications of increasing inequality, and the measurement of economic well-being. Among other professional responsibilities, he has served as President of the Canadian Economics Association.

*Ito Peng* is Professor of Sociology and Director, Centre for Global Social Policy, Department of Sociology, University of Toronto. She has written extensively on family and gender policy, labour market change and the sociology and political economy of care in East Asia. She is the Principal Investigator of a SSHRC-funded research project examining how the reorganization of care influences the global migration of care workers and how such migration influences family and gender relations, gender equality, government policies and global governance. Professor Peng has held several senior administrative positions at the University of Toronto, including Associate Dean, Interdisciplinary and International Affairs; Chair and Director, Dr. David Chu Program in Asia Pacific Studies; and Director, Centre for Studies of Korea.

# Index

www.ingramcontent.com/pod-product-compliance
Lightning Source LLC
Chambersburg PA
CBHW050738030426
42336CB00012B/1622